Ruth and Augustus Goetz

The Heiress

Based on the novel Washington Square
by Henry James

Edited with an Introduction by
E. R. WOOD

HEINEMANN EDUCATIONAL BOOKS
LONDON

Heinemann Educational Books Ltd
22 Bedford Square, London WC1B 3HH

LONDON   EDINBURGH   MELBOURNE   AUCKLAND
SINGAPORE   KUALA LUMPUR   NEW DELHI
IBADAN   NAIROBI   JOHANNESBURG
PORTSMOUTH (NH)   KINGSTON

ISBN 0 435 22300 3

Printed and bound in Great Britain by
J. W. Arrowsmith, Bristol

THE HEIRESS

Based on the novel *Washington Square* by Henry James. The central character is Catherine Sloper, the plain, shy daughter of a distinguished and wealthy New York physician. When a handsome but penniless young man, Morris Townshend, proposes to marry her, Dr. Sloper, regarding him as a fortune-hunter, forbids the match. Catherine, who has never before been treated with tenderness, is determined to elope, but when the suitor hears that she will be disinherited, his ardour cools, and Catherine waits in vain for the sound of his carriage wheels. Two years later, when the doctor has died, Morris reappears, and is delighted to find Catherine apparently ready to forgive and willing to marry him. But her experience of her father and her lover has hardened her, and when Morris drives up to keep his appointment this time, it is her turn to keep him waiting; and he knocks on the locked door in vain.

THE HEREFORD PLAYS

General Editor: E. R. Wood

CONTENTS

INTRODUCTION

The Heiress is described as 'based on' the novel *Washington Square*,* written more than sixty years earlier, by Henry James. The play stands on its own, of course, as a fine example of the art of the dramatist, but it is interesting to consider its source and inspiration in the art of the novelist. By comparing the two works we may clarify in our minds the different qualities expected of novel and play and the different kinds of pleasure which they offer.

Henry James and the Theatre

The case of Henry James is of special interest because of his own persistent but thwarted ambition to succeed as a dramatist. From childhood he was a regular and eager playgoer in New York, Paris and London; he became a dramatic critic with wide knowledge and great authority; he interrupted for a time his career as a novelist so as to write a number of plays, some of which *nearly* succeeded: yet his very distinguished place in English Literature rests on his novels and tales, and where his name is honoured in the theatre of today, it is for dramatic adaptations of his novels by others, rather than for his own plays.

James was both attracted to the theatre and repelled by it. In writing to R. L. Stevenson he expressed both attitudes in the same letter – even in the same sentence. He speaks of his play, *The American*, as 'a tribute to the vulgarest of the Muses', but remarks, 'I find the *form* opens out before me as if it were a kingdom to conquer – a kingdom, forsooth, of ignorant brutes of managers and dense *cabotins* of actors.' He liked the idea of writing drama as a form of literature, but recoiled from submitting his work to the judgement of uncultivated minds. 'I may have been meant for the Drama – God knows!'

* Published by Heinemann Educational Books in the New Windmill Series.

he said after a humiliation by an audience, 'but I certainly wasn't meant for the Theatre!' It was Henry James who first called the theatre 'the Unholy Trade'. In an outburst to his publisher, William Heinemann, he complained that the dramatist must write for the stupid; 'that is, your maximum of refinement must meet the minimum of intelligence of the audience – the intelligence, in other words, of the biggest ass it may conceivably contain'. He grumbled that in order to be understood by an audience composed of people at varied mental levels it was necessary to be crudely explicit, to 'dot one's *i*'s as with pumpkins'. In one of his novels (*The Tragic Muse*) he expresses through one of his characters his own contempt for the Victorian theatre-going public and the hopelessness of trying to write well for them;

> The *omnium gatherum* of the population of a big commercial city at the hour of the day when their taste is at its lowest, flocking out of the hideous hotels and restaurants, gorged with food, stultified with buying and selling and with all the other sordid preoccupations of the age, squeezed together in a sweltering mass, disappointed with their seats, timing the author, timing the actor, wishing to get their money back on the spot. Fancy putting the exquisite before such a tribunal as that! There's not even a question of it. The dramatist wouldn't if he could, and in nine cases out of ten he couldn't if he would. He has to make the basest concessions. One of his principal canons is that he must enable his spectators to catch the suburban trains, which stop at 11.30. . . . What can you do with a character, with an idea, with a feeling, between dinner and the suburban trains? You can give a gross sketch of them, but how little you touch them, how bald you leave them! What crudity compared with what the novelist does!

This passage is a piece of amusingly jaundiced exaggeration, (notice the grossly over-coloured words – 'hideous hotels', 'gorged with food', 'stultified with buying and selling', 'sweltering mass'), but there is a grain of truth in it. And yet, at another moment, Henry James writes from the opposite point of view: 'All the same, I feel as if I had at last found my form – my real one – that for which pale fiction is an ineffectual substitute.'

The Novelist's Art in Washington Square

It is evident that a play which is to be appreciated in a limited time by a heterogeneous audience may have to be less subtle, less delicate – even cruder – than a novel. The texture of a Jamesian novel, what he called 'the figure in the carpet', may be elusive to the rapid glance or the casual eye. One must also miss in the theatre the pleasure to be derived from the novelist's own style – ironical, confiding, all-knowing, treating his characters with indulgence or mockery. When Henry James tells us how Morris Townsend first kissed Catherine, we learn less than in the play about what the pair *said*, but more about how Catherine *felt*. The whole incident – and the light in which Morris and Catherine are to be regarded – comes to us with a colouring of James's irony:

> What Morris told Catherine at last was simply that he loved her, or rather adored her. Virtually, he had made known as much already – his visits had been a series of eloquent intimations of it. But now he had affirmed it in lover's vows, and, as a memorable sign of it, he had passed his arm round the girl's waist and taken a kiss. This happy certitude had come sooner than Catherine expected, and she regarded it, very naturally, as a priceless treasure. . . . After Morris had kissed her, as a ripe assurance of his devotion, she begged him to go away, to leave her alone, to let her think. Morris went away, taking another kiss first. But Catherine's meditations lacked a certain coherence. She felt his kisses on her lips and on her cheeks for a long time afterwards; the sensation was rather an obstacle than an aid to reflection.

The dry flavour of this passage, the Jamesian quality of voice, could not be retained in a dramatized version of the story.

Or consider the occasion when Catherine tells her father

that she is engaged to be married. 'You do right to tell me,' the Doctor answers, exactly as in the play. 'And who is the happy mortal whom you have honoured with your choice?' 'Mr Morris Townsend,' she answers. But the novelist is able to go beyond the range of what can be conveyed on a stage:

> As she pronounced her lover's name Catherine looked at him. What she saw was her father's still grey eye and his clean-cut, definite smile. She contemplated these objects for a moment, and then she looked back at the fire; it was much warmer.

Again, the reader may take a dry pleasure in Henry James's view of Aunt Penniman (which resembles that held by Dr Sloper). He has told us how Catherine, when jilted by Morris, tried to keep her misery to herself. 'How well Catherine deceived her father we shall have occasion to learn,' we read, 'but her innocent arts were of little avail before a person of the rare perspicacity of Mrs Penniman. This lady easily saw that she was agitated, and if there was any agitation going forward, Mrs Penniman was not a person to forfeit her natural share in it. She returned to the charge the next evening, and requested her niece to lean on her – to unburden her heart.' But though 'from hour to hour Mrs Penniman's curiosity grew', we are told that Catherine 'from hour to hour kept her aunt at bay'.

It will be seen from the above examples that the novelist can offer much which has to be sacrificed by the playwright. He also has more time and space. *Washington Square* is more than twice the length of *The Heiress*. The reader can enjoy it at leisure; he can read for an hour or two one evening, reflect on what he has read, look back and re-read if he wishes, go on when he likes at his own pace. The playwright must not only condense his material to make it fit into a shorter time; he must also make it clear and interesting to many different people at the same moment. Something is inevitably lost in the process, but much is gained. The discipline of the medium creates strength; and the situation of actors on a stage before an audience generates an excitement different from that of story-telling. These factors which James resented are essentials which give drama its own quality.

Shaping a play – The Heiress

In one of his pro-theatre moods Henry James once wrote:

> The fine thing in a real drama, generally speaking, is that, more than in any other work of literary art, it needs a masterly structure. It needs to be shaped and fashioned, and laid together, and this process makes a demand upon an artist's rarest gifts. He must combine and arrange, interpolate and eliminate, play the joiner with the most attentive skill, and yet at the end effectively bury his tools and sawdust, and invest his elaborate skeleton with the smoothest and most polished integument.

This is exactly what was done for *Washington Square* by Ruth and Augustus Goetz.

It is worth examining the craftsmanship of the first few pages of the play to notice how skilfully the information is presented, the characters and their relationships are introduced, and the future is prepared for, with every line contributing something significant. In the opening minutes we meet the urbane Dr Sloper and his sister Mrs Penniman, a small-town widow, who is much impressed by staying in Washington Square, New York. They are expecting guests, and we learn that the daughter of the house, Catherine, is a source of anxiety to her father on such occasions. Before Catherine appears we hear that she is gentle and good, but her father would prefer her to be clever. His comment, 'You are good for nothing unless you are clever', is a self-revelation and a a signpost to the alienation ahead. Catherine comes in. She is quite gay and amusing in conversation with her aunt, but there is a sadness: though she is most anxious to please her father, she knows that she is a disappointment to him. When the doctor returns, a chill falls in spite of his courtesy. Catherine had hoped to please him with her new dress, but it creates the first climax of tension in the play; and when she is urged by her aunt to repeat a comic anecdote, all the fun withers before her father's expectant smile. Thus the main theme of the play, Catherine's relations with her father, is now set before us, awaiting development. All is ready for the first appearance of Morris Townsend, who is destined to bring about a concentration of all that is most cruel to Catherine in the world around her.

This is only the beginning of a far-reaching reorganization of Henry James's material which is undertaken throughout the play. An obvious line of refashioning is dictated by the convenience in a theatre of unity of place – in this case making everything happen in the same room in the Doctor's house in Washington Square. For instance, in the novel the party at which Catherine first meets Morris Townsend is held at Mrs Almond's house, and the Doctor inflicts his cynical teasing on the ladies as they drive home in the carriage. Sometimes the alterations of place involve further changes. Thus instead of going to visit Morris Townsend's sister in her modest little house of red brick, as in the novel, Dr Sloper in the play asks her to come to see him in Washington Square. One consequence is that Mrs Montgomery meets Catherine (for the first time) there, sees for herself how inadequate she is as a hostess, and realizes that the attraction for Morris must be (as the Doctor says) her money – for her charms are not the kind to captivate a young man like her brother. Her motives become different. In the novel her talk with the doctor stirs her bitterness against her brother, so that she says firmly, 'Don't let her marry him!': in the play (having met Catherine) she is touched by her simplicity and gentleness, and offers the doctor more compassionate advice: 'If you are so opposed to the marriage, then, as a father, you must find a kinder way of stopping it.' She then leaves. Having changed not only the scene of the doctor's interview with Mrs Montgomery, but also its tenour and outcome, the playwrights have presented themselves with an effective theatrical moment, when Catherine comes back from the kitchen with a tray of refreshments, only to find that the visitor has gone. It poignantly emphasizes Catherine's lack of self-confidence, which both saddens and exasperates her father.

Again, the European tour, which fills one chapter of the novel, becomes in the play a mere blank between Acts One and Two. Much more is made by the playwrights of the actual return, and here we see very clearly the different purposes and methods of novel and play. Morris Townsend is seen at his ease at the backgammon board with Mrs Penniman, enjoying the doctor's cigars and brandy, until they are both startled by the sound of a carriage stopping outside, bringing home the returning travellers unexpectedly soon. This scene, a complete invention by Ruth and Augustus Goetz, is a concentration into ten minutes of stage time of the tensions and conflicts diffused over several days in the novel. Before it ends Catherine has realized how coldly her father despises her and she knows that she must expect nothing from him. The elopement proposed by Morris seems therefore justifiable – the sooner the better. All is now planned ready for the highly dramatic climax that is to follow – the jilting.

The difference between novel and play could hardly be more emphatically underlined than in the treatment of the jilting of Catherine. In the novel, there is nothing in prospect so dramatic or romantic as an elopement; Morris becomes gradually convinced that Dr Sloper will cut Catherine out of his will if they marry, so he loses interest in the affair; he deliberately provokes a quarrel with Catherine, tells her that he has to go away on business, and will not commit himself to calling again. Catherine is bewildered, stunned, overwhelmed with grief. But, we are told by the novelist:

She said to herself that perhaps he would come back to tell her he had not meant what he said; and she listened for his ring at the door, trying to believe that this was possible. A long time passed, but Morris remained absent; the shadows gathered; the evening settled down on the meagre elegance of the light, clear-coloured room; the fire went out. When it had grown dark, Catherine went to the window and looked out; she stood there for half an hour, on the mere chance that he would come up the steps. At last she turned away, for she saw her father come in. He had seen her at the window looking out, and gravely, with an air of exaggerated courtesy, lifted his hat to her.

This is vivid and even dramatic story-telling, but for stage purposes most of it has to be jettisoned, only the picture of Catherine waiting for the ring at the door being used as the germ of a new scene. In the play the tension of the young girl waiting in vain for her lover to drive up and carry her off is built up to a climax when the clock strikes one and she realizes that Morris has failed her.

It will be noticed that in the story, as related by James, Catherine is alone while she waits, and afterwards will not tell anyone – especially not Aunt Penniman – what has happened. But when the incident is elaborated and presented on the stage, Catherine has to make her sufferings not only visible but audible to somebody, so Mrs Penniman is brought into the scheme and the scene, contributing a few wounding shafts to the dialogue.

Having created the splendid theatrical effect of waiting for the lover's ring at the door, the playwrights were only human to exploit its possibilities a second time with a wry difference; so at the end of the play Catherine has her revenge when Morris rings and it is Catherine's turn to let *him* w t in vain. This repetition, with the tables turned, gives a satisfying shape to the theatrical experience. The point is much less strongly made in *Washington Square*. There is nothing so clearly defined as a revived elopement plan – not surprisingly, since very many years have elapsed. Morris is now forty-five, no longer the straight, slim young man who had so enchanted Catherine once. She admits him very unwillingly and never for a moment encourages his rather tentative advances. 'I can't begin again – I can't take it up,' she says. 'Everything is dead and buried. It was too serious; it made a great change in my life. I never expected to see you here.' Morris accepts total rebuff, and goes out, indignant with Mrs Penniman for having encouraged him to come. 'She doesn't care a button for me – with her confounded dry manner', he exclaims as he strides out of the house. Catherine gives him his deserts in a matter-of-fact, undramatic way, and Henry James ends the novel on a very unemphatic note: 'Catherine, meanwhile, in the parlour, picking up her morsel of fancy work, had seated herself with it again – for life, as it were.' Thus it will be noticed that the two most dramatic and memorable scenes in the play are interpolations, which the fastidious Henry James might have regarded with distaste as examples of 'dotting the i's as with pumpkins' to suit the flat-footed public. 'What crudity,' he might have said, 'compared with what the novel does!' Yet at another time he said that the process 'makes a demand on the artist's rarest gifts'.

Characterization

In characterization, as well as in construction, the dramatist must condense, simplify and bring into sharp focus. The character must become clear to the audience from what he says and does; the playwright cannot provide little comments, amusingly confided, like the following analysis of Catherine's attitude to her father and her lover:

> There were probably people in the world as bad as her father supposed Morris to be, and if there were the slightest chance of Morris being one of those sinister persons, the Doctor was right in taking it into account. Of course, he could not know what she

knew, how the purest love and truth were seated in the young man's eyes; but Heaven, in its time, might appoint a way of bringing him to such knowledge. Catherine expected a good deal of Heaven, and referred to the skies the initiative, as the French say, in dealing with her dilemma. She could not imagine herself imparting any kind of knowledge to her father; there was something superior even in his injustice and absolute in his mistakes. But she could at least be good, and if she were good enough, Heaven would invent some way of reconciling all things – the dignity of her father's error and the sweetness of her own confidence, the strict performance of her filial duties and the enjoyment of Morris Townsend's affection.

In the play, as in the novel, there is an uncomfortable occasion when Catherine comes in wearing a new dress. Her father says, 'Is it possible this magnificent person is my daughter?' A stage direction tells us that 'Catherine does not know quite how to take this.' The novelist is able to give more than this hint; he enriches our understanding of the relationship between father and daughter in a sprightly style not possible for the playwright:

> You would have surprised him if you had told him so, but it is a literal fact that he almost never addressed his daughter save in the ironical form. Whenever he addressed her he gave her pleasure, but she had to cut her pleasure out of the piece, as it were. There were portions left over, light remnants and snippets of irony, which she never knew what to do with, which seemed too delicate for her own use; and yet Catherine, lamenting the limitations of her understanding, felt that they were too valuable to waste, and had a belief that if they passed over her head they yet contributed to the sum of human wisdom.
> 'I am not magnificent,' she said mildly, wishing that she had put on another dress.

In the play a more chilling touch is added when Dr Sloper suggests that the colour is wrong for Catherine, though it would have been right for her beautiful and brilliant mother, with whom poor Catherine is often compared to her disadvantage.

What is interesting in stage character is development. In *The Heiress* both Catherine and her father change more definitely than in *Washington Square*, as a result of the strains and conflicts arising from the Townsend affair. At the beginning of both, the Doctor is an intellectually refined, emotionally arid man, recognizing his duty as a father, but often irritated by Catherine. Even when she declines to accept his shrewd estimate of Morris, he tries to remain patient. He takes her to Europe, though her company is no pleasure to him, in the hope that she will get over her infatuation. It is from the failure of this move that a new development takes a firmer line than in the novel. Catherine is as obstinate as ever, and he no longer conceals his contempt for her. He says more deeply wounding things to her in the play, but he is also more capable of compassion at times, perhaps because he is ill, and the prospect of dying makes him more human. When Catherine is at the crisis of her suffering, he is aware of it and tries to offer his sympathy and (thinking it is she who has had the strength to break with Morris) his admiration. Even when she tells him harshly that it is Morris who has jilted *her* (in the novel she keeps her father guessing) he is touched with pity, saying, 'My poor child!' But Catherine has no mercy. She turns from him, saying bitterly, 'Don't be kind, father. It does not become you!' and when he asks her not to withhold her natural affection, she answers, 'I have no affection for you, father.' This is a case where the conflict is greatly sharpened and the emotions are excited to make a strong dramatic scene. In the novel, there is no such confrontation. Dr Sloper remains cold and on the whole pleased with the outcome. When he sees that his daughter is in distress, 'he might have pitied her', Henry James writes, 'and, in fact, did so; but he was sure he was right'. Being right, about Morris is a satisfaction he clings to while his daughter is needing tenderness. He watches with what he himself calls 'genial curiosity' to see whether Catherine will 'stick', so that Mrs Almond says to him, 'You are shockingly cold-blooded.' Later he has the pleasure of telling his sister that 'the scoundrel has backed out' and adds, 'I had foretold it. It is a great pleasure to be right.' Mrs Almond, realizing what Catherine must be going through comments, 'Your pleasure make me shudder.'

There is no clearly defined moment in the novel when the Doctor is made to see what Morris and he have between them done to Catherine. She is so determined to hide her trouble from her father, and she is so successful – or he is so insensitive – that he tells Mrs Almond there is nothing wrong with her:

> She eats and sleeps, takes her usual exercise, and overloads herself, as usual, with finery. . . . She hasn't much to say; but when had she anything to say? She has had her little dance, and now she is sitting down to rest. I suspect that, on the whole, she enjoys it.

They live on together without affection, but without recrimination, for years. The Doctor goes again to Europe for two years, and takes Catherine and Aunt Penniman with him. She never mentions Morris, and he is never quite sure that the danger is over for good, but when he asks her to promise him that she will never marry Morris she refuses. He tells her that he is about to alter his will, but she remains obstinate. A year later he catches cold and develops congestion of the lungs. He gives the same instructions for the nursing as in the play (but he does nothing so theatrical as using his stethoscope on himself) and dies after a three weeks' illness, during which Catherine is 'assiduous at his bedside'. After his death it is found that his will has been altered to cut Catherine's legacy to one-fifth of what it was, but Catherine is content.

Drama thrives on emotion, on crisis, and on conflicts. The Dr Sloper of the play offers more scope to the actor and evokes emotional response from the audience because he is a little warmer. He has more moments of compassion, and more clear-cut confrontations; having killed his daughter's affection, he finally feels a need for it. In the novel the emotion is toned down or concealed, and spread over many more years.

The case of Catherine illustrates the same points about the differences between novel and play. In the novel she never talks much, and after the Morris affair (as has been indicated) she makes a policy of hiding her feelings under a placid surface, and saying very little that would make effective dialogue on the stage. Her inadequacy as a talker is analysed by Henry James in his account of her behaviour after Morris Townsend has called in Washington Square the second time. She feels uncomfortable about telling her father he has been. She blurts it out abruptly, and then is about to leave the room. 'But she could not leave it fast enough,' we are told; her father stopped her as she reached the door.

> 'Well, my dear, did he propose to you today?' the Doctor asked. This was just what she was afraid he would say; and yet she had no answer ready. Of course she would have liked to take it as a joke – as her father must have meant it; and yet she would have liked, also, in denying it, to be a little positive, a little sharp; and for a moment she only stood, with her hand on the door knob, looking at her satiric parent, and giving a little laugh.
>
> 'Decidedly,' said the Doctor to himself, 'my daughter is not brilliant!'

Catherine finally thinks of something to say. She says, 'Perhaps he will do it next time,' but by the time she gets to her own room she is wishing he would ask her the question again, for she has thought of something sharper to reply.

The Catherine of *Washington Square* remains stolid and matter-of-fact (decidedly not brilliant) to the end. In her last encounter with Morris she says nothing more eloquent than 'You treated me badly' and 'Please don't come again'. But in *The Heiress* she develops more ruthlessness in character and a gift of speech which makes powerful theatre. When her father is mortally ill she describes so eloquently the wrong he did her that he says, 'You have found a tongue at last, Catherine. Is it only to say such terrible things to me?' Her answer expresses all her bitter experience, with cold irony worthy of the doctor himself: 'Yes, father. This is a field in which you will not compare me with my mother.' When Aunt Penniman is startled by Catherine's treatment of Morris at the end, she sums up the essence of the play in her reply, 'Yes, aunt, I can be cruel. I have been taught by masters.'

'What can you do with a character . . . between dinner and the suburban trains?' *The Heiress* shows that you can do a good deal, but the conditions of the theatre may impose a more positive line of development to a more emphatic conclusion.

Dialogue

The authors of *The Heiress* were remarkably clever at writing dialogue which, while retaining the flavour of Henry James, makes a stronger impact on an audience. Not that dialogue was a weakness of James. On the contrary, the reader of his novels is often struck by the dramatic quality of the conversations, and there are sometimes whole pages of *Washington Square* which have been incorporated word for word in *The Heiress*. But it must be said that almost all the really memorable lines in the play, especially those in which Catherine so forcefully answers her father and her aunt, belong to the theatre, and are not to be found in the novel.

Conclusions

The reader who has become familiar with *The Heiress* will find it fascinating to turn to its source, and to study in detail the differences of emphasis and intention. *Washington Square* is an absorbing but rather astringent novel: *The Heiress* says what it has to say more effectively, perhaps more movingly.

But does it say the same thing?

Of course the two versions have much in common. Both record the harm done to a rather plain, innocent girl by a cold-blooded, egocentric father and a calculating fortune-hunter. The essence is summed up in the novel:

> From her point of view the great facts of her career were that Morris had trifled with her affection, and that her father had broken its spring. Nothing could ever alter these facts; they were always there, like her name, her age, her plain face. Nothing could ever undo the wrong or cure the pain that Morris had inflicted on her, and nothing could ever make her feel towards her father as she had felt in her younger years.

The Townsend affair is a sort of catalyst in her relations with her father: it reveals that he has never loved her. She doesn't blame him for this. 'You can tell when a person feels that way,' she says in the novel. 'I don't accuse him; I just tell you that that's how it is. He can't help it; we can't govern our affections. . . . It isn't my fault, but neither is it his fault.'

There is no doubt in either version that Dr Sloper was right in his assessment of Morris Townsend. Was he not right, then, to stop the marriage by threatening to deprive the pair of the one thing that mattered to Morris – the prospect of riches? The question is answered in *The Heiress*:

> SLOPER: Some day you will realize I did you a great service.
>
> CATHERINE: I can tell you now what you have done; you have cheated me. If you could not love me, you should have let someone else try.
>
> SLOPER: Morris Townsend didn't love you, Catherine.
>
> CATHERINE: I know that now, thanks to you.
>
> SLOPER: Better to know it now than twenty years hence.
>
> CATHERINE: Why? I lived with *you* for twenty years before I found out that *you* didn't love me. I don't know that Morris would have cheated me or starved me for affection more than you did.

There is nothing so explicit in *Washington Square*, where Catherine goes on living for nearly twenty years more with the father who does not love her; but she keeps her resentment to herself. 'There was something dead in her life', we read, 'and her duty was to fill the void. Catherine recognized this duty to the utmost; she had a great disapproval of brooding and moping.'

What is remarkable in the novel is the degree to which she is able to survive the pain and resume a quiet, unemotional relationship with her father and her aunt. There is very little disturbance of her placid surface even when Morris reappears long after. 'She would never have known him . . . it seemed to be he, and yet not he; it was the man who had been everything, and yet this person was nothing.' For his part, he has no idea what she once suffered. 'You had your quiet life with your father,' he reminds her, 'which was just what I could not make up my mind to rob you of.' In fact, the affair has died a slow death.

But such quiet ends are not the stuff of drama.

NOTE ON THE AUTHORS

Henry James was born in New York in 1843, and educated in Europe and at Harvard. He lived much of his life in England, and became a British citizen shortly before his death in 1916. *Washington Square* was first published in 1881.

Ruth Goodman was born in Philadelphia and educated in New York and Paris. She married Augustus Goetz and collaborated with him in writing plays and adaptations. *The Heiress* was first published under the title *The Doctor's Daughter* in 1945.

CAST OF FIRST LONDON PERFORMANCE

The Heiress was first produced in England at the Theatre Royal, Haymarket, on the 1st February, 1949, directed by Sir John Gielgud.

CAST

DR SLOPER	Ralph Richardson
CATHERINE	Peggy Ashcroft
MORRIS TOWNSEND	James Donald
LAVINIA PENNIMAN	Gillian Lind
MRS MONTGOMERY	Ann Wilton
ELIZABETH ALMOND	Madge Compton
MARIAN ALMOND	Gillian Howell
ARTHUR TOWNSEND	Donald Sinden
MARIA	Pauline Jameson

CHARACTERS

DR SLOPER
CATHERINE, *his daughter*
MORRIS TOWNSEND
LAVINIA PENNIMAN
MRS MONTGOMERY

ELIZABETH ALMOND
MARIAN ALMOND
ARTHUR TOWNSEND
MARIA

SCENES

The entire action of the play takes place in the front parlour of Doctor Sloper's house in Washington Square. The year is 1850.

ACT ONE
SCENE ONE: *An October evening*
SCENE TWO: *An Afternoon two weeks later*
SCENE THREE: *The Next morning*

ACT TWO
SCENE ONE: *An April night six months later*
SCENE TWO: *Two hours later*
SCENE THREE: *A morning three days later*
SCENE FOUR: *A summer evening almost two years later*

ACT ONE

The scene is the drawing-room of Dr Sloper's handsome home in Washington Square. Two windows on the right look out on to the Square. They are in line with the front door of the house, which opens into the foyer. Upstage this foyer is divided from the drawing-room proper by pillars of the period, which outline the archway. The staircase can be seen beyond. On the left of the room is the fireplace and above it a door which leads into the Doctor's study. In front of the fireplace is Dr Sloper's chair with a small table beside it. In the centre of the room, facing the audience, is a love seat; behind it there is a centre table, to which are drawn up a few occasional chairs. On the right, near the windows, is another chair with Catherine Sloper's embroidery frame standing to one side of it. On the back walls on either side of the archway stand two Duncan Phyfe settees. Between the windows there is a table with flowers, an oil lamp, and a small miniature of Dr Sloper's wife.

The house is not decorated in the gaudy Victorian style which we have come to associate with all nineteenth-century interiors. Dr Sloper set up housekeeping with his young bride in 1820, and he and she were in a position in life to buy Duncan Phyfe's furniture, and to combine it with the English mahogany which their forebears had brought with them. His tastes have certainly not changed in the years which have elapsed since that time, and so the house which he built himself in Washington Square is furnished with discretion and elegance. Only in the elaborate drapes and hangings that mask the doors and windows and arches does the new taste for opulence betray itself, and even that, in Dr Sloper's home, is modified. The mantelpiece, the crystal chandelier, the mirror over the mantel, the Gilbert Stuart family portraits of Mrs Sloper's family, these are the indications of the Doctor's affluence.

The time is October evening in 1850. MARIA, *a parlour maid, is lighting the ornate kerosene lamps. We hear a carriage pass in the street. As* MARIA *adjusts the wick of the last lamp the front door of the house opens, and then closes. She goes to the archway.*

MARIA: Good evening, Doctor.

DR SLOPER (*his voice in the hallway*): Good evening, Maria. (*He enters the room. He is a distinguished middle-aged man, impeccably dressed and pleasant in manner.* MARIA *takes his hat, and then he crosses to a table where he sets down a small medical bag. She stands beside him as he removes his gloves.*)

MARIA: Would you like your supper now, Doctor?

DR SLOPER (*surprised*): Have Miss Catherine and her Aunt waited for me?

MARIA: No, sir. They dined quite early. They wanted plenty of time to dress.

DR SLOPER (*remembering*): Oh, yes – (*He glances at the clock.*) Well, our company won't be here for a while.

MARIA: No, sir. Cook has kept everything warm. Can I bring you a tray?

DR SLOPER: No, thank you, Maria, I had a little something at the Garrisons'.

MARIA: How is Mrs Garrison?

DR SLOPER: She is fine ... fine ... She is the mother of a new citizen. (*He sits down with a trace of weariness.*) He and I shook hands for the first time at exactly a quarter-past six. (MARIA *goes to a side table where she pours a glass of sherry for Dr Sloper.*)

MARIA: It's a boy?

DR SLOPER (*sipping sherry*): Yes.

MARIA: How nice. They wanted a boy, didn't they?

DR SLOPER: They just wanted a child, Maria, and now they've

got one – eight and a half pounds. Such beautiful little creatures ... Why don't they grow up that way? (*Another sip.*) Maria, when you marry, you must have a lot of children. Don't put all your hopes on one. (*Sips.*)

MARIA (*smiling*): That's what my mother said ... she had thirteen.

DR SLOPER: Where is my daughter, Maria?

MARIA: Miss Catherine is upstairs, sir.

DR SLOPER (*rises*): I must register that birth. Oh, Maria, Mr Garrison will come by at the side door later tonight for a copy of the document. I'll leave it out for you.

MARIA: I'll see that he gets it, sir.

  MRS LAVINIA PENNIMAN *comes down the stairs. She calls out* –

MRS PENNIMAN: Is that you, Austin? (*She enters the room. She is a middle-aged lady in somewhat coquettish mourning.*)

DR SLOPER: Good evening, Lavinia.

MRS PENNIMAN: How nice that you are home! I was afraid the baby might take all the evening, and then our little party would be spoiled.

DR SLOPER: No, the baby kept his engagement promptly.

MARIA (*as she is about to leave*): Excuse me. What time shall I serve the collation, Doctor?

DR SLOPER: What time did Miss Catherine suggest?

MARIA: She said, to ask you.

DR SLOPER: ⎱ Well, I should ...
MRS PENNIMAN: ⎰ Serve it ..

MRS PENNIMAN: Serve it late! (*Then embarrassed at her effrontery.*) Well, I would like a long visit with Sister Elizabeth. And I'm anxious to get to know Marian's young man.

DR SLOPER (*pleasantly*): Serve it late, Maria.

MARIA: Yes, sir. (*She goes out.*)

MRS PENNIMAN (*anxious to tell*): Austin, I had the most exciting time today!

DR SLOPER (*surprised*): With Catherine?

MRS PENNIMAN: Oh, no, Catherine was busy. I went out alone (*She sits down and prepares to tell an exciting story.*) Now you might not approve of this, but I strolled into the Astor Hotel all by myself.

DR SLOPER (*amused*): Lavinia! What a daring thing to do. How did you like the oil paintings over the bar?

MRS PENNIMAN: The bar? Oh, Austin! Shame on you! I didn't go there to drink – I wanted to see the grand staircase. Oh, a birth certificate! and as I stood there admiring it, I heard a voice behind me saying, 'Isn't that Lavinia Penniman?' I turned around, and who do you suppose it was?

DR SLOPER: Could it have been a fellow Poughkeepseian?

MRS PENNIMAN: Two of them!

DR SLOPER: Good gracious, what a windfall!

MRS PENNIMAN: They had been members of my husband's congregation. And do you know – they have not set foot in that church since he passed away. They said it would be hard to fill the Reverend Penniman's place in the community.

DR SLOPER (*meditatively*): Yes – he was a large man . . .

MRS PENNIMAN: And then they asked me where I was stopping, and when I told them with my brother, Dr Sloper at 16 Washington Square, they were so impressed! It's just made my visit!

DR SLOPER: Then you couldn't have told them what a dreary time we're giving you.

MRS PENNIMAN: Oh, Austin, you're not. I've enjoyed being with you and Catherine.

DR SLOPER: Have you really, Lavinia? Have you enjoyed it enough to stay on? I have been wondering if you'd care to spend the winter here?

MRS PENNIMAN (*pleased*): Here? . . . Would you like me to?

DR SLOPER: Yes. I have been asked to represent our doctors at a medical congress in Paris in December.

MRS PENNIMAN (*deeply impressed*): Paris, France?

DR SLOPER (*smiles*): Yes. (*Resumes his thought.*) Of course Catherine is of an age where she can perfectly well stay alone with the servants, but I thought if you lived here while I was away, you might help her.

MRS PENNIMAN: Help her . . .? But help her how, Austin? She goes out very little, she hardly needs me as a chaperone. She runs this house most competently. She obviously doesn't want a confidante, so what am I to help her to?

DR SLOPER: Well, for instance, this evening while our company is here – perhaps you could persuade Catherine to remain quietly in the room with us and join in the conversation?

MRS PENNIMAN: But, Austin, of course she will do that!

DR SLOPER: The last time I had guests she disappeared into the pantry four successive times.

MRS PENNIMAN: Oh! Well, I will try, Austin. And, of course, I will gladly stay the winter.

DR SLOPER: Good! Now, my dear, if you will excuse me, I must go and dress. (*He starts to the study, but half-way he turns back to her.*) Help her to be clever, Lavinia. I should so like her to be a clever woman.

MRS PENNIMAN: But she is so gentle and good!

DR SLOPER (*at the door*): You are good for nothing unless you are clever! (*He exits.*)

> *Left alone,* MRS PENNIMAN *goes over to the window and stares out. As she is thus occupied,* CATHERINE SLOPER *descends the stairs and enters the room. She is a healthy, quiet girl in her late twenties. She is dressed in an over-elaborate red satin gown with gold trimmings.*

MRS PENNIMAN: Catherine. (*She turns into the room.*) Oh, you've got it on!

CATHERINE: Yes. Do you like the colour?

MRS PENNIMAN: Yes, it's extremely rich.

CATHERINE: Do you think Father will like it?

MRS PENNIMAN: He's bound to. You know, one of the last times I ever saw your poor mother, she was wearing the most delicious little bows of that colour in her hair.

CATHERINE: Yes, Aunt, I know. You said they were cherry red.

MRS PENNIMAN: So they were.

CATHERINE: I picked it up at the dressmaker's on my way to the Hospital Committee this afternoon. The ladies all thought it was a lovely colour. Is father in his study?

MRS PENNIMAN: No, he's upstairs dressing. Tell me about the meeting! Did you have a nice time?

CATHERINE: Some of the women are so foolish that they are funny. They think it ill-bred to know anything about food, so they are useless on the Committee. One girl asked me today if veal was the front or the hind part of the cow.

MRS PENNIMAN (*smiling*): What did you tell her?

CATHERINE (*with humour*): Well, Aunt, I told her the truth. I said it was a nursing calf, and just when it was most adorable, most touching . . . we *eat* it!

MRS PENNIMAN (*laughs*): Such airs and graces! When I was young we took pride in our housewifery. When I think of the meals I used to set before the Reverend Penniman . . .

CATHERINE (*teasing*): Then you have deceived me, Aunt!

MRS PENNIMAN (*surprised*): How so?

CATHERINE: You led me to believe that you and he lived on love alone! (*They laugh.*)

MRS PENNIMAN (CATHERINE *is about to go to the study door, when* MRS PENNIMAN *stops her. She is embarrassed*): Oh, Catherine! Catherine, dear . . . er . . . since you are so handsomely dressed you will allow Maria to attend to all the details of the collation this evening?

CATHERINE: They are already attended to.

MRS PENNIMAN: Good! Then you won't have any reason to go into the pantry – will you?

CATHERINE (*A pause*): You have been talking to Father.

MRS PENNIMAN: Well, in a way – I have. You see, dear, your father feels . . .

CATHERINE: Father would like me to be composed and to direct the conversation.

MRS PENNIMAN: Yes.

CATHERINE: But I can't. That is why I go into the pantry.

MRS PENNIMAN: But, dear, perhaps you do not try sufficiently?

CATHERINE: Oh, I do, I do. I would do anything to please him. There is nothing that means more to me than that. (*Confidingly.*) I have sat upstairs sometimes and thought of things I should say, and how I should say them, but when I am in company – I lose it all.

MRS PENNIMAN: But why, Catherine? With me you express yourself on every subject.

CATHERINE: When I am here in the parlour with Father, it seems that no one could want to listen to *me*. No matter what I have thought about upstairs, down here it seems so unimportant.

MRS PENNIMAN: Well, Catherine, if you will observe your cousin Marian this evening you will see that what she says is never of any great consequence, but that doesn't keep her from saying it.

CATHERINE: Yes, Aunt, but Marian might recite the alphabet, and Arthur Townsend would still think her the cleverest girl in New York.

MRS PENNIMAN: Are you envious of Marian, Catherine?

CATHERINE: Why, I have never even met Mr Townsend!

MRS PENNIMAN: I don't mean in that way. I mean, shouldn't you like to be an engaged girl, too?

CATHERINE: I don't know. The question has never come up.

MRS PENNIMAN: Not even in your own mind? Don't you

ever think about having your own home and husband and children?

CATHERINE (*very quietly*): Yes, I think about it.

MRS PENNIMAN: Well, don't you desire it?

CATHERINE (*hesitant*): It is the *person* I think of. It is to find someone to love.

MRS PENNIMAN: And someone who loves you.

CATHERINE (*simply*): But that is the same thing.

    There is a moment's pause. DR SLOPER *comes downstairs.*

DR SLOPER: Ah, Catherine. Good evening, my dear.

CATHERINE: Good evening, Father. Do you like my dress?

DR SLOPER (*eyeing her fully*): Is it possible this magnificent person is my daughter? (CATHERINE *doesn't know quite how to take this.*) You are sumptuous, opulent . . . You look as if you had eighty thousand dollars a year.

CATHERINE: I thought you would like the colour . . .

DR SLOPER: Hm'm.

CATHERINE: It is cherry-red . . .

DR SLOPER: Ah'a!

CATHERINE: My Mother used to wear it.

MRS PENNIMAN: In her hair ribbons . . .

DR SLOPER: Oh yes, Catherine, but your mother was dark – *She* dominated the colour.

    CATHERINE *goes to her embroidery frame.* MRS PENNIMAN *sensing tension, tries to mend matters.*

MRS PENNIMAN: Catherine was at a meeting of the Ladies' Hospital Committee today, Austin.

DR SLOPER (*to* CATHERINE): Oh, really?

MRS PENNIMAN: She has been very active there all the week.

DR SLOPER: Good! How do you like it, my dear?

CATHERINE: Very much. It is very stimulating.

DR SLOPER: That's fine. I like women who do things. What is your particular duty?

CATHERINE: I copy out the vegetable lists for the Children's Ward.

DR SLOPER: Well, that's necessary work. (*He indicates her embroidery.*) Are you starting another of those samplers?

CATHERINE: Why, yes, Father. I find it a most agreeable pastime.

DR SLOPER: Don't let it turn into a life work, Catherine.

MRS PENNIMAN (*again stepping into the breach*): Catherine had such a amusing experience at the Hospital today, Austin. (*Turns to her.*) Catherine, dear, tell your father about that young woman. Tell him, just the way you told me.

DR SLOPER (*with an expectant smile*): Yes, please do.

CATHERINE: Well ... er ... there was a young woman – er – also on the Committee and she asked me about veal ...

DR SLOPER: Yes?

CATHERINE: ... she didn't know what it was.

DR SLOPER: I see. .?

MRS PENNIMAN (*eagerly*): She thought it was part of the cow, didn't she, Catherine?

CATHERINE: Yes ... she didn't know it was calf.

DR SLOPER: She didn't?

CATHERINE (*struggling*): She didn't know any of the cuts of beef.

DR SLOPER (*waiting*): I see ...

MRS PENNIMAN: You see, Austin, Catherine told her it was a *young* cow.

DR SLOPER: Yes ...?

CATHERINE (*lost*): Well, I just thought that ... that she might not have liked it.

DR SLOPER: Ah ... (*Indicating her position as she sews.*) That is not a very good light for sewing, Catherine; you might hurt your eyes. (*The doorbell rings.*)

CATHERINE: Yes, Father.

MARIA *crosses the hall to the front door.* MRS PENNIMAN *rises.*

MRS PENNIMAN: Here they are! (*She goes into the hall.*)

MARIA (*in the hall. We hear her voice as she admits the guests*): Good evening, Mrs Almond.

MRS ALMOND (*a voice in the hall*): Good evening, Maria ... Livvie!

MRS PENNIMAN (*a voice in the hall*): Lizzie!

MARIA (*voice in the hall*): Good evening, Miss Marian.

MARIAN: Good evening, Maria.

> MRS ALMOND, *a handsome woman in her forties, appears in the archway.*

MRS ALMOND: Good evening, Austin ... Hello, Catherine dear.

DR SLOPER: How nice to see you, Liz. (*He draws her into the room.*)

MRS ALMOND: Well, Austin, who's ill? Who's dead? Whom have you been cutting up lately?

DR SLOPER (*amused*): Ah, I see you are in good health, Liz. You're more respectful to me when your gout's troubling you.

MRS ALMOND: Arthur, this is my brother, Doctor Sloper. (ARTHUR *bows.*) And this is Marian's cousin, Catherine.

ARTHUR: How do you do, Miss Sloper.

> MARIAN ALMOND *enters. She is a pretty, vivacious girl in her early twenties.*

MARIAN: Good evening, Uncle Austin.

DR SLOPER: Marian, my dear, how nice to see you!

MARIAN (*crossing to* CATHERINE *and embracing her*): Hello, Cathie!

> *Another young man,* MORRIS TOWNSEND, *appears in the archway next to Arthur. He is a handsome, lively man in his late twenties.*

CATHERINE: Good evening, Marian.

ARTHUR: How do you do, Doctor? I have taken the liberty of bringing my cousin. I thought that since you were meeting me, you wouldn't mind meeting him. (*He turns to* MORRIS *in the archway.*) Morris, meet Doctor Sloper. Doctor Sloper, Morris Townsend.

MORRIS: How do you do, Sir.

MRS PENNIMAN (*as she enters the room and passes* MORRIS *at the archway*): And *I* am the Doctor's other sister.

MORRIS (*bows*): How do you do, ma'am. (*As he advances towards Dr Sloper.*) I hope you will pardon my intrusion on a family party, Doctor and Miss Sloper. I am newly returned from Europe and feel somewhat lost.

DR SLOPER: I am delighted to meet you, sir ... (*To Arthur.*) You did quite right to bring your cousin.

MARIAN: How grand you look, Cathie! I told Morris he should find you very grand, and then he was determined to come! (*She sits on the settee at the back wall.*)

ARTHUR: Marian (*beckoning her over*).

CATHERINE (*shyly, and holding on to Dr Sloper's arm with both hands*): Thank you, Marian. (*To Arthur.*) How do you do, sir? (*To Morris, with an identical bow.*) How do you do, sir.

DR SLOPER: No, Catherine ... (*He loosens one of her hands from his arm.*) The young gentlemen cannot take chairs until you do.

CATHERINE: I'm sorry, Father. (*She sits down at the centre table.* MORRIS *sits across from her at the same table.* ARTHUR *sits next to Marian.*)

MARIAN: Uncle Austin, Arthur says that a house in Washington Square is the best investment in the city.

DR SLOPER (*to Arthur*): I am happy to see that we think alike, sir.

ARTHUR: Er ... yes ... the counting house with which I am associated thinks very highly of the Square. We have funds available for mortgages at all times.

DR SLOPER: Well ... that's most reassuring.

MRS PENNIMAN: And when is the marriage to be, Marian?

MARIAN: The twentieth of November, Aunt Lavinia. Arthur wanted to hold me off till spring, but I wouldn't have it!

MORRIS: Arthur will have the truest cause to celebrate Thanksgiving of his life!

MRS PENNIMAN: How charmingly expressed, Mr Townsend!

MORRIS (*to Catherine*): I hear from Miss Almond that you are to be one of the bridesmaids, Miss Sloper?

MARIAN: Bridesmaid! Why, Cathie's to be my maid of honour!

MRS PENNIMAN: Perhaps Catherine will catch the bride's bouquet!

MRS ALMOND: Of course she will. Marian will aim it at Catherine. They can practice with a bean bag.

There is some polite laughter, CATHERINE *is nervously twisting her handkerchief.* DR SLOPER *rises and goes to her.*

DR SLOPER (*picking the handkerchief out of her hand and putting it in his pocket; he gives Catherine a cue*): Mr Morris Townsend has lately returned from Europe, Catherine.

CATHERINE: Have you been away long, sir?

MORRIS: Yes, I have, to my disadvantage, as I now see.

CATHERINE: Why?

MORRIS: I find that I have missed some lovely things at home.

CATHERINE (*faintly*): Oh!

MORRIS: Besides, people forget you.

MARIAN (*teasing*): He wants us to say that we would never forget him, don't you, Morris?

CATHERINE (*protesting*): Oh, Marian . . .

MORRIS (*smiling*): There is nothing I would rather hear. (*To Catherine.*) Are you as great a tease as your cousin, Miss Sloper?

CATHERINE: No. (*She rises, and the young men rise with her.*)

DR SLOPER: Is there something I can get you, Catherine?

CATHERINE (*trapped, she sits down again*): My embroidery.

DR SLOPER: We will admire it later, my dear.

MORRIS: Ah, Miss Sloper, you are just like the young ladies of Paris. They, too, are always busy with their 'petit-point.' (*He pronounces the last word with a good French accent.*)

MRS PENNIMAN (*ecstatically*): Oh! You speak French!

MORRIS: A little, ma'am.

DR SLOPER: Did you make the Grand Tour, Mr Townsend?

MORRIS: No, sir. I spent most of my time in France, and Italy.

MRS PENNIMAN: Italy! Oh, how beautiful it must be!

MORRIS: You don't know it, ma'am?

MRS PENNIMAN: No, I've never been there, but I have always felt it must be the most romantic country. Such handsome men and such beautiful women! Tell me, Mr Townsend, do you find our American young ladies very different?

MORRIS: So different, ma'am. (*He looks at Catherine expressively.*) So delightfully different!

    CATHERINE, *in a spasm of nervousness, knocks over a miniature on the table.*

DR SLOPER: It's all right, Catherine.

CATHERINE (*trying to straighten it*): I didn't break it, Father!

DR SLOPER (*calming her*): Of course you didn't, dear. (*Then quickly, in order to draw away the attention.*) Mr Townsend, I suppose I shall find Paris unchanged?

MORRIS: Are you planning a trip, sir?

DR SLOPER: I hope to attend a medical congress there this winter.

MRS ALMOND: It's a tremendous trip, Austin, just to go and talk to a lot of other doctors.

DR SLOPER (*smiling*): Oh, between talks I shall find time for other things. I shall walk in every street I walked in the first time many years ago; I shall shop in every shop . . .

MORRIS: And smell every smell . . .? (*They laugh.*)

MORRIS: I see you really love the city, sir!

DR SLOPER: I have good reasons to . . . I went there on my wedding trip.

MARIAN: We have been having a wonderful time listening to all the new French songs. We kept Morris playing for hours last evening.

MORRIS: I don't know how you stood it!

ARTHUR: Oh, come now, Morris, don't be modest!

MARIAN: Would you like to hear some, Cathie?

(CATHERINE *doesn't answer.*)

MRS PENNIMAN: I should love to!

ARTHUR (*looking around*): Too bad, Morris, no pianoforte.

MORRIS (*gaily*): Oh, what a pity! (*Then confidentially to Catherine.*) And it's my trump card, Miss Sloper.

MRS PENNIMAN: There is a spinet in the study.

CATHERINE (*appalled*): But that was Mother's!

DR SLOPER: The instrument is not in tune.

MORRIS: I do not play well enough, sir, for that to make much difference.

DR SLOPER (*firmly*): I'm sorry.

MRS ALMOND: Let them try it, Austin. I haven't heard music here in a long time.

MRS PENNIMAN: Please, Austin.

ARTHUR: He wants to outshine me, Doctor, with the ladies.

DR SLOPER: Very well, Lavinia, if you wish it.

MRS PENNIMAN (*rises and starts for the study*): This way, Mr Townsend. (*She goes out to the study.*)

MARIAN *and* ARTHUR *follow Mrs Penniman.*

MARIAN: Let us use some of our wedding money for a fine pianoforte, Arthur. (*They go out.*)

MORRIS, *with great alacrity, gets to the small kerosene lamp just as Catherine does.*

MRS PENNIMAN (*returns*): Catherine, dear, bring the lamp. There is none on the spinet.

MORRIS: Please allow me, Miss Sloper. It might be too heavy for you.

CATHERINE (*trying to hang on to it, as* MORRIS *tries to relieve her of it*): Oh, no!

MORRIS: Please . . . (*But* CATHERINE *still hangs on to it.*)

CATHERINE: It's quite all right . . .

DR SLOPER: Catherine! (*With controlled irritation.*) Let the young man carry it for you!

CATHERINE (*relinquishes it*): Yes, Father. (*She goes into the study.*)

MORRIS (*following her*): You thought I was going to drop it, didn't you, Miss Sloper? I *won't*. I shall be most careful.

After they have left, DR SLOPER *goes to the small table, picks out a cigar, lights it, and then rejoins Mrs Almond.*

DR SLOPER: I will never understand it. Her mother was so graceful!. . .

MRS ALMOND, *embarrassed, looks away.* MRS PENNIMAN *re-enters from the study.*

MRS PENNIMAN: Austin, Mr Townsend can't open the spinet! Is it locked?

DR SLOPER (*he takes the key from his waistcoat pocket*): Here is the key, Lavinia. See that I get it back.

MRS PENNIMAN: Thank you. (*Then confidentially.*) Isn't he charming? (*She goes out.*)

DR SLOPER: She does *not* mean Arthur, Elizabeth.

MRS ALMOND: I know she doesn't.

DR SLOPER: What about this cousin? Who is he?

MRS ALMOND: He's a *distant* cousin, it seems. Arthur's mother is always talking about branches of the family: elder branches, younger branches, inferior branches, as if it were a royal house. Now, Arthur, it appears, is on the royal line, his cousin Morris is not.

We hear a song being played on the spinet in the study.

DR SLOPER: Cousin Morris has a royal ease about inviting himself along, hasn't he? Quite the sort of figure to please the ladies.

MRS ALMOND: Yes.

DR SLOPER: Did he do anything before he went on his travels?

MRS ALMOND: I don't think so. I believe he had a very small inheritance. He intimated that he had used it up. He lives in the Second Avenue with his sister.

DR SLOPER: Who is she?

MRS ALMOND: A Mrs Montgomery, a nice little woman, a widow. I met her once at a charity bazaar for needy children. She has five of her own.

DR SLOPER: A widow, with five children? Do you mean he lives *on* her?

MRS ALMOND: I can hardly answer that, Austin. You would have to ask her. Tell me . . . what do you think of Arthur?

DR SLOPER (*smiling*): Arthur . . .? Well, he isn't very lively, is he. I see him as the president of a bank at fifty.

MRS ALMOND: Good!

DR SLOPER: A small bank.

MRS ALMOND: Even so, Marian will like that.

DR SLOPER: Are you entirely satisfied with the arrangement?

MRS ALMOND (*shrugs*): She wanted him.

DR SLOPER: Do you suppose there is another Arthur somewhere in this great city of ours?

MRS ALMOND: Oh, Catherine will find a husband!

DR SLOPER (*amused*): Do you think so?

MRS ALMOND (*impatiently*): She has the prospect of thirty thousand a year.

DR SLOPER (*smiling*): I see that you appreciate her.

MRS ALMOND: I don't mean it's her *only* merit. You always have a way of alluding to her as an unmarriageable girl!

DR SLOPER: You see how she is with young men.

MRS ALMOND: That is the trouble in New York; the men are too young. They marry at the age of innocence, before the age of calculation. If they only waited a little, Catherine would fare better.

DR SLOPER: As a calculation? Thank you very much!

MRS ALMOND: Of course, I didn't mean it that way!

DR SLOPER (*shrugs*): We need not deceive each other, my dear.

MRS ALMOND: Austin, are you really as detached as you seem about Catherine?

DR SLOPER: Detached? That's the last thing I am! I am deeply

interested in every phase of her life. Detached! Hah, I wish
I were!

MRS ALMOND: Why?

DR SLOPER: Because I wish I could have confidence in her
ability to manage herself, and her future, with some
wisdom, or even some intelligence.

MRS ALMOND: I see that you have no confidence and I
imagine that Catherine sees it, too.

DR SLOPER: If you are reproaching me, Liz, you must be more
specific. What would you like me to do for her that I have
not done? Is there something that I have missed? She has
been to the best schools in the city. She has had the finest
training I could get her in music and dancing. She has sat
here with me evenings on end, and I have tried to make
conversation with her, and give her some social adeptness.
She has never been constrained in the spending of money,
or in the direction of the household. I have given her free-
dom wherever I could. The result is what you see . . . an
entirely mediocre and defenceless creature with not a shred
of poise. What did I do wrong, my dear sister? If you know
I wish you would tell me, for *I* do not.

MRS ALMOND: I do not mean that you have not done your
duty as a father.

DR SLOPER: I have been as good a father as it was possible for
me to be with the material Providence gave me.

The music starts again in the study. They listen for a moment.

MRS ALMOND (*surprised*): Why, it *is* in tune, Austin!

DR SLOPER: Yes.

MRS ALMOND: That's quite remarkable, after all these years.

DR SLOPER: I keep it looked after. I have a man who comes in
three or four times a year.

MRS ALMOND: You should encourage Catherine to play.

DR SLOPER (*sharp*): I do. She can't.

MRS ALMOND: Austin, you are so intolerant! And you *expect*
so much!

DR SLOPER: Yes, I expect everything! You remember her mother, Liz. Her mother, who had so much grace and gaiety! Her mother, who was such a pleasure to look at and be with! This is her child ... (*He pauses.*) I was entitled to expect that some day she would make it up to me, wasn't I?

MRS ALMOND: Make what up?

DR SLOPER: Her mother's death! She killed her mother in getting born.

MRS ALMOND (*pityingly*): Oh, Austin!

DR SLOPER: I have lived these years in loneliness, waiting for Catherine to be all the lovely things her mother was. I let nothing interfere with it. I did not marry. I did not do anything to endanger the process. I concentrated my life on seeing her approach the perfection of her mother!

MRS ALMOND (*severe*): No child could compete with this image you have of her mother. You have idealized that poor dead woman beyond all human recognition!

DR SLOPER (*outraged*): You are not entitled to say that! Only *I* know what I lost when she died (*The music swells. They listen.* MRS ALMOND *watches Dr Sloper.*) When I hear that spinet played, I remember the day she got it ... We were in Paris and she bought it at Pleyel's. She wouldn't sail for home until she found a captain who was willing to let her take it on board with her. Six months later she was dead.

MRS ALMOND (*gently*): That was a long time ago, Austin.

DR SLOPER: That is no consolation.

　　As they listen to the music, the lights dim and the

CURTAIN FALLS

It is a sunny afternoon two weeks later. The drawing-room is brilliant with the sunlight from the Square, and there is an Indian Summer quality in the light which makes the room seem very cheerful.

MRS PENNIMAN *and* MORRIS TOWNSEND *are together on the settee, and* MRS PENNIMAN *is laughing as the curtain rises.*

MRS PENNIMAN: Really, Mr Townsend, you shouldn't make fun of Arthur. After all, he is your relative!

MORRIS: I don't care about that! But he did introduce me into this house, and for that I must be grateful all the rest of my life . . . (*He bows his head to her gracefully.*) Here I have found a true friend . . .

MRS PENNIMANN (*she looks into the hallway*): Perhaps you have found something more important than that in this house?

MORRIS: Did you tell her that I would call today?

MRS PENNIMAN: I must confess that I did not. She is so gentle, so timid, I was afraid she would take flight at your third visit within the week.

MORRIS: There's nothing special about three visits, is there? And since she's out anyway, what have we gained?

MRS PENNIMAN: She will be home, I am sure of it.

MORRIS: Well, but when?

MRS PENNIMAN (*pleased with his impatience*): Ah, Mr Townsend, you remind me so of the Reverend Penniman. The same ardency, the same passionate nature.

MORRIS (*resigning himself*): Was she pleased with the flowers, Mrs Penniman?

MRS PENNIMAN: I think very pleased.

MORRIS: What did she say?

MRS PENNIMAN (*flatly*): She said, 'They are a spring flower. It is unusual to get them so late.'

MORRIS: Is that all?

MRS PENNIMAN: But she took them upstairs to her sitting-room and placed them right next to her chair at the window. I think that's good, don't you?

MORRIS: What did her father say?

MRS PENNIMAN: How do you mean?

MORRIS: Did he tease her when he saw them?

MRS PENNIMAN: How would he see them? He never goes into her sitting-room.

MORRIS (*pumping*): Does Catherine – I mean, Miss Sloper —?

MRS PENNIMAN (*smiling*): My boy, you may let yourself go when you are with me.

MORRIS: Does Catherine see many young men, Mrs Penniman?

MRS PENNIMAN (*embarrassed*): Er – Well, she receives many invitations. And she always attends the Cotillions.

MORRIS: I don't mean that. I mean does she receive young men like myself, often?

MRS PENNIMAN: She is of a retiring nature.

MORRIS: I cannot believe that she is so reserved with everybody. I am afraid she disapproves of me.

MRS PENNIMAN (*in alarm*): Oh, no.

MORRIS: She gives me no encouragement . . .

MRS PENNIMAN: But that is because she is so shy.

MORRIS: Oh dear, then we shall never know her heart, shall we?

MRS PENNIMAN: She is not shy with *me*, Mr Townsend. She confides in me freely. In the privacy of her own room she is very expressive.

MORRIS: Dare I ask what my name has brought forth in that privacy?

MRS PENNIMAN: I can assure you that she has a wealth of feeling, but she is wary of showing it.

MORRIS (*musing*): It's odd. In Europe a girl like that would have been married long since. Why, in Paris, with her income, she might have got a Count!

MRS PENNIMAN (*enchanted*): A Count? Do you really think so? (*Remembering.*) But Austin would never have it!

MORRIS: Tell me about the Doctor, ma'am. What are his interests? Does he like art or paintings? Has he any hobby?

MRS PENNIMAN: His work is his hobby. Medicine is his only mistress.

MORRIS: That's a devil of a difficult thing for a man like me to talk about!

MRS PENNIMAN: Once he knows what is going on in your heart, you will have plenty to talk about between you! (*We hear the front door open, then close.* MRS PENNIMAN *holds up her finger warningly to Morris.*) Catherine, is that you?

CATHERINE: Yes, Aunt.

MRS PENNIMAN: You have a visitor, young lady. He has been waiting for your return most anxiously.

CATHERINE (*now in the drawing-room*): Good afternoon . . .

MORRIS: It is a beautiful afternoon for me now, Miss Sloper. But I was afraid you might not come back at all.

CATHERINE: Oh, I should have to come back some time. I live here.

MORRIS (*smiling*): I know you do, Miss Sloper. That's why I am here — (*There is a slight pause.*)

MRS PENNIMAN: Mr Townsend wondered if his flowers had been delivered in good condition?

CATHERINE: Yes, thank you! They were very fresh. I mailed a note to you this morning.

MORRIS: I shall treasure it, Miss Sloper, although I did not send the flowers in order to be thanked. (*He looks at Mrs Penniman rather severely.*) I sent them to give you pleasure.

CATHERINE: Thank you.

MORRIS: Oh, I found the poem I told you about.

CATHERINE: Did you?

MORRIS: I am such a vagabond – I've left it in my hat! Pardon me, ma'am. I'll get it. (*He goes into the hall, while the two women look at each other in the drawing-room.*)

MRS PENNIMAN (*conspiratorial*): I will leave you alone with him.

CATHERINE: What will I talk about?

MRS PENNIMAN (*smiling*): You will not have to do the talking. My dear child; he has come a-courting!

CATHERINE: Do you mean courting me!

MRS PENNIMAN: Certainly not me, Miss . . . (*She kisses her.*) You must be very gracious to him.

MORRIS *returns with the poem, on a sheet of paper.*

MORRIS: I copied it off late last night. (*He looks at Catherine expressively.*) I was restless and could not sleep.

MRS PENNIMAN: Mr Townsend, you must excuse me. I have numerous duties which call me. I trust that we shall see you again.

MORRIS (*bowing low*): I am your servant, ma'am.

MRS PENNIMAN: Catherine, don't forget to rest before going out, for tonight. (*To Morris.*) Our girl is off to another one of her endless parties tonight, Mr Townsend! Dancing . . . dancing till dawn . . . (*She goes out.*)

MORRIS: It makes me very unhappy to hear that.

CATHERINE: What?

MORRIS: That you are so gay, so sought after. It makes my way harder.

CATHERINE: Oh, but I am not going to a party tonight. My father and I are dining with Mr and Mrs Hone. That is all.

MORRIS: That's what I like about you, you are so honest. (*As if embarrassed.*) Will you tell me something, Miss Sloper? . . . Did you go out today because you thought I might call?

CATHERINE (*after a pause*): Yes.

MORRIS: Do you not like to see me?

CATHERINE: Yes, I like to see you, Mr Townsend. But you have called so frequently this week that I —

MORRIS (*smiling*): You are tired of me!

CATHERINE: No.

MORRIS: You consider my behaviour improper?

CATHERINE: I do not know. I am puzzled.

MORRIS (*laughing*): Good! I like that! If you are puzzled, you are thinking of me, and that is what I want above all; that you should think of me.

CATHERINE: Mr Townsend, you are very bold.

MORRIS (*confidently*): I will be bolder; I will ask you one more question. Miss Sloper, when you came back just now, did you hope that I would be gone – or – that I would be here?

CATHERINE (*averting her eyes*): Is that the poem?

MORRIS (*gaily*): It is. I had forgotten it. I forget everything when I find myself here with you! (CATHERINE *holds out her hand for it.*) It says the things I tried to say to you the last time I was here.

CATHERINE: May I read it?

MORRIS: Oh, not now! Perhaps you will read it when you are alone. It will say more to you then. (*He gives it to her. She takes it and stares at it.*) I will think of you reading it when I stand under your window.

CATHERINE: Oh, Mr Townsend, you must not do that!

MORRIS (*mocking her gently*): Oh, Miss Sloper, how am I to help doing it? I think of you constantly.

CATHERINE: I am not very good at this kind of conversation.

MORRIS: Neither am I. I am afraid that is our trouble – I am not a glib man, Miss Sloper.

CATHERINE: Oh, but I think you talk very well.

MORRIS: Never when I need it most, never when I am with you. Oh, when I'm with Mrs Penniman, or in my room at home, I can think of the most delightful things to say — Can you understand that?

CATHERINE: Yes, I can.

MORRIS: But here, with you, I sound like a fool.

CATHERINE (*smiling*): I don't think so.

MORRIS: Well, if ever you should think so, if ever I have sounded high-flown or false, put it down to that, will you?

CATHERINE: I will try.

MORRIS: And take pity on my situation.

CATHERINE: What situation?

MORRIS: Miss Sloper, I have fallen in love with you.

CATHERINE (*with a gasp*): You have?

MORRIS: You are breathless —

CATHERINE: Yes, I am.

MORRIS: Why . . . is it so strange?

CATHERINE: Yes, it is very strange.

> *During the preceding,* DR SLOPER *has come in the front door and removed his hat in the hall. He sees Morris's hat.*

DR SLOPER: Ah, Catherine, are you receiving?

CATHERINE: Yes, Father. I have a visitor.

DR SLOPER (*enters the drawing-room*): Good afternoon, my dear. How do you do, Mr Townsend?

MORRIS: Good afternoon, Dr Sloper.

DR SLOPER (*looking around*): Is your cousin here with you? (*To Catherine.*) Where's the happy couple?

CATHERINE: They are not here, Father.

MORRIS: I took the liberty of coming on my own, sir. I wanted to thank Miss Sloper and yourself for having received me the first time.

DR SLOPER: That's most polite, sir. It was a very small gathering and we were pleased to have you.

MORRIS (*gracefully*): Sometimes it is the small parties at which one takes the greatest pleasure. This one gave me an excuse to call on a most attractive young lady, and her attractive father.

DR SLOPER: Oh, we are not that attractive. Catherine, will you pull the bell? I'd like my sherry and biscuits. Mr Townsend might enjoy some with me.

MORRIS: I'd be honoured.

> CATHERINE *crosses and pulls the bell.*

DR SLOPER (*sniffing*): That's an excellent bay rum you are using, Mr Townsend.

MORRIS: I brought it with me from France, Doctor. Permit me to share it with you.

DR SLOPER: Why in the world should you?

MORRIS: There is no reason, sir, except the pleasure it would give me.

DR SLOPER: I could hardly allow you to do that. (*Settling down, and addressing Catherine.*) Well, Catherine (*She does not hear.*) Catherine! (*He claps his hands.*) What have you been up to, my dear? Did you decide to do anything further about the music lessons?

CATHERINE: Yes, Father, I called on Mr Rougini after lunch.

DR SLOPER: And what did he say?

CATHERINE: He said the harp was a very difficult instrument.

DR SLOPER: Well, we both know that, my dear. What else did he say?

CATHERINE: He did not think I was suited to it.

DR SLOPER: Why not?

CATHERINE (*timidly*): You need a true ear for the harp. It seems that I have not a very true ear.

DR SLOPER: Nonsense, my dear, that's impossible. Your mother's ear was impeccable. Why, she used to tune her own pianoforte!

CATHERINE (*looking in her lap*): Yes, Father, I know.

MORRIS (*tactfully*): Miss Sloper has a great appreciation for music. That is a sufficient talent in itself.

DR SLOPER: Do you find it so? (MARIA *enters with the sherry and biscuits.*) Good afternoon, Maria.

MARIA: Good afternoon, Doctor.

DR SLOPER: Is Cook's knee any better?

MARIA: It is a little easier, Doctor.

DR SLOPER (*pouring the sherry*): I'll be up to see her in a little while. Here, give this to Mr Townsend.

MARIA (*offers Morris the wine*): She's not upstairs, Doctor, she's in the kitchen.

DR SLOPER: This is hopeless, Maria! How am I to get rid of the inflammation unless you keep her in bed?

MARIA: Perhaps you'll talk to her, Doctor?

DR SLOPER: I'll be down, as soon as I finish this.

MARIA: Thank you, sir. (*She sets down her tray and exits.*)

MORRIS: You are a very kind man, sir. Most great doctors are too busy to see the illness under their noses.

DR SLOPER: Mr Townsend, you are full of agreeable and flattering observations, both for Catherine and myself. I wonder why?

MORRIS: That is the way you both strike me, sir. I told Miss Sloper earlier – I am very candid.

CATHERINE (*she addresses Dr Sloper but looks at Morris*): Yes, he is very candid.

DR SLOPER (*taking a sip of his sherry*): How do you keep busy since your return to New York, Mr Townsend? Are you looking for a position?

MORRIS: Oh, a position is more than I should presume to call it! That sounds so fine. I should like some quiet work . . . anything to turn an honest penny.

DR SLOPER: What sort of thing should you prefer?

MORRIS: You mean what am I fitted for? Very little, I am afraid. I have nothing but my good right arm, as they say in the melodramas.

DR SLOPER: You are too modest. In addition to your good right arm you have a very good mind. I know nothing of you but what I see; but I see that you are extremely intelligent.

CATHERINE (*murmuring*): Oh, yes – yes!

MORRIS: I don't know what to answer when you say that. (*Looking right at Dr Sloper.*) You advise me then, not to despair?

DR SLOPER (*with a smile*): I should be sorry to admit that a robust, well-disposed man need ever despair. If he doesn't succeed in one thing, he can try another. Only, he should choose with discretion.

MORRIS: Ah, yes, with discretion. Well, I have been indiscreet formerly, but think I have got over it. I am very steady now ... (*Now he smiles.*) Were you kindly intending to propose something to my advantage?

DR SLOPER: No, I have no particular proposal to make. But occasionally one hears of opportunities. I hear, for instance, the West is opening up. Many young men are turning their eyes in that direction.

MORRIS: I'm afraid I shouldn't be able to manage that. I must seek my fortune here or nowhere. You see, I have ties here. (*He turns to Catherine.*) I have a widowed sister from whom I have been separated for a long time, and to whom I am everything.

CATHERINE: Naturally.

MORRIS (*smiling*): I shouldn't know how to tell her that I must leave her. She depends on me so much.

DR SLOPER: That's very proper; family feeling is very proper. I think I have heard of your sister.

MORRIS: It is possible, though I rather doubt it; she lives so very quietly.

DR SLOPER: As quietly, you mean, as a lady may who has several young children?

MORRIS: Yes, my nephews and nieces – that's the very point. I am helping to bring them up. I'm a sort of amateur tutor; I give them lessons.

DR SLOPER: That's very proper, but it's hardly a career.

MORRIS: No, it won't make my fortune.

DR SLOPER (*incisively*): Ah! You must not be too much bent on a fortune ... (*He stands up.*) But I will keep you in mind, Mr Townsend. Be sure I will not lose sight of you. (*He turns to Catherine.*) Catherine, I'm going downstairs (CATHERINE *rises.* DR SLOPER *moves for bag.* MORRIS *hands it to him.*)

DR SLOPER: Oh, thank you. Good afternoon, Mr Townsend.

MORRIS: Good afternoon, Doctor. I am very grateful for your interest.

DR SLOPER: Yes . . . yes, indeed. (*He goes into the hall and starts back along it, presumably to the back quarters of the house. After he has left, the young people remain quiet. Then* MORRIS *speaks first.*)

MORRIS: He doesn't like me – he doesn't like me at all. Extraordinary man!

CATHERINE: I don't see why you should think that.

MORRIS: I feel; I am very quick to feel.

CATHERINE: Oh, no. I am sure you are mistaken.

MORRIS. Well, you ask him, and you will see.

CATHERINE (*slowly*): I would rather not ask him, if there is any danger of his saying what you think.

MORRIS: It wouldn't give you any pleasure to contradict him?

CATHERINE: I never contradict him.

MORRIS (*goes closer to her*): Would you hear me abused without opening your lips in my defence?

CATHERINE: Oh, he won't abuse you. He doesn't know you well enough . . . (MORRIS *laughs.*) . . . I shall simply not mention you.

MORRIS: That is not what I should have liked you to say. I should have liked you to say, 'If my father doesn't think well of you, what does it matter?'

CATHERINE: But I couldn't say that! It *would* matter.

MORRIS: Do you know, I think you could? I think you could do anything for one whom you loved!

CATHERINE (*rising*): Mr Townsend, you mustn't speak to me this way. I mustn't listen to this . . .

MORRIS (*comes close to her and pleads passionately*): It is two weeks since first I saw you, and I have not had an easy moment since that night! I think of nothing else! I am possessed by you!

CATHERINE (*with a desperate sincerity*): How could you be? How could you?

MORRIS: My dearest girl, my whole life depends on your believing me, believing how much I care for you! You are everything I have ever yearned for in a woman!

CATHERINE: But I am so . . . (*Before she can finish, he draws her to him and kisses her.*)

MORRIS: Will you marry me, Catherine?

CATHERINE (*looks at him fully, for the first time*): Yes.

MORRIS (*smiling at her*): You make me very happy . . . Do you love me?

CATHERINE: Yes.

MORRIS (*kisses her again*): Dear Catherine.

CATHERINE: I love you! I love you!

MORRIS: I will cherish you for ever.

CATHERINE (*detaching herself*): We must do our duty. We must speak to my father. I will speak to him tonight. You must speak to him tomorrow.

MORRIS: It is sweet of you to do it first. The young man, the happy lover, usually does that. But just as you please . . .

CATHERINE (*smiles bravely*): Women are more tactful. They can persuade better.

MORRIS: You will need all your powers of persuasion. (*He looks at her.*) But then, you are irresistible!

CATHERINE: Morris, promise me one thing. When you speak to my father, you will be very respectful.

MORRIS: I shall try. I certainly would rather have you easily than have to fight for you.

CATHERINE: Don't speak of fighting; we shall not have to fight.

MORRIS: We must be prepared. After all, it's natural for your father to want a brilliant marriage for you; you have everything – position, wealth, and your own sweetness. And I am a poor man, Catherine.

CATHERINE: Oh, Father will not mind that.

MORRIS: He might. He might fear that I am mercenary.

CATHERINE: Mercenary!

MORRIS: It's a big word, but it means a low thing – that I only want your money.

CATHERINE: Oh, no!

MORRIS: He may say it.

CATHERINE: But that is easily answered. I should simply say that he is mistaken.

MORRIS: You must make a great point of that, Catherine.

CATHERINE: Why.

MORRIS: Because it is from the fact of your having money that our difficulties are likely to come.

CATHERINE (*drawing away from him momentarily*): Morris, are you very sure you love me?

MORRIS: My own dearest, can you doubt it?

CATHERINE: I have only known it for five minutes, but now it seems to me that I could never do without it.

MORRIS: You shall never be called upon to try. (*He kisses her lightly on the cheek.*) . . . Now, there is something you must tell me, too . . . (*He pats her hand.*) You must tell me that if your father is against me, if he even forbids our marriage, you will still be faithful, no matter what comes.

CATHERINE: Yes, Morris . . . No matter what comes.

MORRIS: You know you are your own mistress – you are of age.

CATHERINE: I love you. I will always love you.

MORRIS: My dear girl . . . I will leave you now. But I will be back in the morning to call on him.

CATHERINE: Yes, Morris. At what time?

MORRIS: At eleven sharp.

CATHERINE: I will tell him. You will be punctual, Morris.

MORRIS: Never fear, my love. When I want something badly, I am on the dot! (*He kisses her, then looking up at her, says*): Be your own sweet self, and you will melt him. (*He goes quickly into the hall, picks up his hat, and leaves.*)

CATHERINE *follows him to the door. The door closes and we see* CATHERINE *start to run up the stairs. Half-way up she is met by* MRS PENNIMAN, *who stops her on the stairs.*

MRS PENNIMAN: He has left. Oh, Catherine, is he not charming?

CATHERINE: Yes, Aunt. (*Trying to escape her.*) I must go to my room.

MRS PENNIMAN: Without telling me what he said!

CATHERINE: I must speak to Father.

MRS PENNIMAN: But Catherine, *I* am your natural confidante!

CATHERINE: Yes, Aunt, but I must speak to Father first. I promised Morris I would.

MRS PENNIMAN: Ah, so you call him Morris, now!

CATHERINE: Yes, Aunt, I call him Morris, now. (*She would continue up the stairs, but* DR SLOPER *enters from the back of the house.*)

DR SLOPER: Ah, Catherine, has our guest taken his leave?

CATHERINE: Yes, Father. Is Cook's knee better?

DR SLOPER: Somewhat.

CATHERINE (*with resolution*): Father! May I speak to you privately in ten minutes?

DR SLOPER (*with humour*): Yes, I think I could make such an engagement.

CATHERINE: I will be down promptly. (*She goes up the stairs.* DR SLOPER *stares after her. He turns into the drawing-room.*)

DR SLOPER: Well, Lavinia. Did you know that we had a caller? (*He starts for his study.*)

MRS PENNIMAN: Why, my dear, you can't see the door for him! He has been here *three* times this week!

DR SLOPER (*stops short*): Has he indeed?

MRS PENNIMAN: Yes, isn't it wonderful?

DR SLOPER (*arrested*): What's wonderful about it?

MRS PENNIMAN: Why, Austin, be sensible! He is a charming young man! I never dreamed that he'd be this interested in Catherine!

DR SLOPER: Nor did I. Why hasn't Catherine told me about these visits?

MRS PENNIMAN: I think she feared at first that it might all come to nothing. But this afternoon when he and I were alone together, he spoke of her in terms that were unmistakable. He is devoted to her!

DR SLOPER: What do you know of Mr Townsend?

MRS PENNIMAN: He has told me a great deal about himself. In fact, his whole history. I'm sure he will tell it all to you, and you must listen to him kindly.

DR SLOPER: I think I shall request him very kindly to leave Catherine alone.

MRS PENNIMAN (*surprised*): But why? Oh, I'm sure his intentions are entirely honourable!

DR SLOPER: You think he is sincere?

MRS PENNIMAN: Deeply sincere! I can tell that by the things he has told me; he has bared his very soul to me.

DR SLOPER: Indeed! And revealed exactly what?

MRS PENNIMAN: Well, he frankly confesses that he has been wild. But he has paid for it, Austin!

DR SLOPER: Does that account for his impoverishment?

MRS PENNIMAN: I don't simply mean in terms of money. He is very much alone in the world.

DR SLOPER: Why? He has a devoted sister, and half a dozen nephews and nieces!

MRS PENNIMAN: The nephews and nieces are all children, and the sister is not a very sympathetic person.

DR SLOPER: I hope he doesn't abuse her to you, for I am told he lives on her!

MRS PENNIMAN: Lives on her?

DR SLOPER: Lives with her and does nothing for himself; it's the same thing.

MRS PENNIMAN: But he is looking for a position most earnestly. He hopes every day to find one.

DR SLOPER: Do you suppose he is looking for it here, Lavinia, in this front parlour?

MRS PENNIMAN: What can you mean, Austin?

DR SLOPER: Wouldn't the position of husband to a defenceless young woman with a large fortune suit him to perfection?

MRS PENNIMAN (*shocked*): Austin! How can you entertain such a suspicion?

DR SLOPER: Suspicion? It is a diagnosis, my dear.

MRS PENNIMAN: You are not in your clinic. This is not a matter for diagnosis. You have only to use your eyes, which are as good as mine!

DR SLOPER: Better.

MRS PENNIMAN: Well then, you must see that Morris Townsend would be a feather in any girl's cap. He's a gentleman. He is handsome and likeable and he is far and away the most eligible man that ever came into Catherine's life! You should be delighted with this courtship.

DR SLOPER: Well, before I become too delighted, I should like to understand it a little better.

MRS PENNIMAN: Let me tell you, Austin, I know a great deal more about these things than you do . . . You don't need to understand it. Just be thankful that it has come at all.

CATHERINE *comes down the stairs and enters the room.*

CATHERINE: I am here, Father.

DR SLOPER: Yes, Catherine, my dear. Come in.

CATHERINE (*looking at Mrs Penniman*): Aunt Penniman . . .

MRS PENNIMAN: Would you like to see your father alone, dear?

CATHERINE: If you wouldn't mind.

MRS PENNIMAN: Not at all, Catherine. (*She pats her on the shoulder as she passes.*) Not at all . . . (*She goes out.*)

DR SLOPER (*after they are alone*): Well, Catherine, you have something to tell me?

CATHERINE: Yes.

DR SLOPER: I shall be very happy to hear it, my dear. Do you suppose that we might both sit down?

CATHERINE (*she sits down on the chair nearest to her. There is an uneasy pause while he waits. Then she blurts out her news*): I am engaged to be married!

DR SLOPER: You do right to tell me. (*Watches her.*) And whom have you honoured with your choice?

CATHERINE: Mr Morris Townsend.

DR SLOPER: When was this arrangement made?

CATHERINE: Here, this afternoon.

DR SLOPER: Before I sat with you both, or after?

CATHERINE: Oh, after.

DR SLOPER (*lights a cigar*): You have gone fast.

CATHERINE: Yes, I think we have.

DR SLOPER: And you are fond of Mr Townsend?

CATHERINE: I like him very much, of course, or I should not have consented to marry him.

DR SLOPER: Mr Townsend ought to have waited and told me.

CATHERINE: He means to tell you tomorrow morning at eleven o'clock.

DR SLOPER: It is not quite the same thing, my dear. You should not be pleading for him. He should plead for you!

CATHERINE: Yes, Father, but I think he is – a little afraid of you.

DR SLOPER: Is he?

CATHERINE: He fears that you do not like him.

DR SLOPER: Well, I hardly know him, Catherine, but our liking each other is not important. The only thing that is important is that he loves you.

CATHERINE: Yes, Father, that is what he feels. He so fears to have you think him mercenary.

DR SLOPER (*abruptly he lays down his cigar*): Mercenary! What an odd word for you to use, Catherine!

CATHERINE: It is not my word, Father, it is his.

DR SLOPER: Is it, indeed? He does not flatter either of us by using it.

CATHERINE: Father, he is a poor man, and I think that has made him sensitive.

DR SLOPER: Yes, I understand that. But there are many poor men, Catherine, and they do not go through the streets proclaiming that they are not thieves. Especially when no one has accused them.

CATHERINE: Father, you must try to understand him. He loves me, and I love him. What has happened is very important to me.

DR SLOPER: It is important to both of us.

CATHERINE (*gently*): Yes, Father, but not equally. My whole happiness is at stake.

DR SLOPER: I think you exaggerate.

CATHERINE: No, Father, I do not. It is a very great wonder to me that Morris has come into my life. I never expected to meet a man who would understand me as perfectly as he does.

DR SLOPER: You underestimate your many qualities, my dear. Well, I have always hoped that some day you would meet a fine young man who would match your goodness with his own.

CATHERINE (*smiling*): And here I have found the goodness, and with it everything else! Oh, Father, don't you think he is the most beautiful young man you have ever seen?

DR SLOPER: He is very good-looking, my dear, Of course, you would not let a consideration like that sway you unduly —

CATHERINE: Of course not! But that's what is so wonderful to me, that he should have everything, everything that a woman could want – and he wants me!

DR SLOPER (*decisively*): Well . . . I will see him tomorrow.

CATHERINE (*happily*): I knew you would. And you are so good that you will be fair and honest with him.

DR SLOPER (*slowly*): I shall be as fair and honest with him as he is with you.

CATHERINE (*rises to leave him*): Thank you, Father. That is all we shall need. (*She goes up the stairs.*)

DR SLOPER *stares after her for a second, then deliberately goes over and pulls the bell cord. Now he goes to the archway and gets his silk hat. He comes back into the room to look at the clock on the mantel, as* MARIA *enters.*

DR SLOPER: I am going out, Maria; I must make a call immediately.

MARIA: Oh, but Doctor, there is a patient waiting for you in your office!

DR SLOPER (*he gives this some thought, then goes to the centre table where there is a writing-case and pen*): Then you must deliver a note for me.

MARIA: Yes, Doctor.

DR SLOPER (*with his hat still on his head, he sits at the table*): It is for – (*he writes*) a Mrs Montgomery who lives in the Second Avenue. (*Continues to write.*) You will have to go to my sister, Mrs Almond, and she will give you the exact address. (*He still writes.*) When you get to Mrs Montgomery's, see that it is delivered directly into her hand.

MARIA: Yes, Doctor.

DR SLOPER (*finishing the note*): You had better take a hack, both ways. (*He folds the note and hands it to her as he rises.*) Here you are. (*He takes some silver out of his waistcoat pocket.*)

MARIA: Thank you, Doctor. (DR SLOPER, *head bowed and deeply preoccupied, starts for his study.* MARIA *stops him.*) Your hat, sir.

DR SLOPER (*turns abstractedly, then as he remembers, he removes it and hands it to her*): Eh? . . . Oh, yes . . . yes . . . *He goes into his study as the –*

CURTAIN FALLS

Ten o'clock in the morning of the following day. The room is empty.
DR SLOPER *opens the front door and enters the parlour. He*
carries his medicine case and wears his hat. He compares his watch
with the mantel clock. He puts his hat on the table in the hall.
MARIA *enters from the kitchen.*

MARIA: Is anything wrong, Doctor?

DR SLOPER (*going to his study*): No, Maria.

MARIA: You're home so early from the Clinic.

DR SLOPER: I have an appointment here. (*He returns to the*
parlour.)

MARIA (*indicating the gloves in her hand*): Oh! These are Mr
Townsend's gloves. He left them here yesterday afternoon.
(*She hands them to Dr Sloper. The doorbell is heard.*) Are you
at home, sir?

DR SLOPER: I am, indeed, Maria! If Mr Townsend should call
while I am engaged, please show him into my office. (DR
SLOPER *puts gloves on centre table as* MARIA *goes out to front*
door.)

MARIA: Yes, Doctor?

(*Off stage.*) Good morning, Mrs Almond.

MRS ALMOND (*off-stage*): Good morning, Maria.

MARIA (*off-stage*): Doctor Sloper is in the front parlour,
ma'am.

MRS ALMOND (*to Mrs Montgomery off-stage*): This way, Mrs
Montgomery. (*She enters the drawing-room.*) Good morning,
Austin.

DR SLOPER: 'Morning, Liz.

MRS ALMOND (*bringing Mrs Montgomery forward*): Mrs
Montgomery. This is my brother, Dr Sloper. Mrs Montgomery has been good enough to come, Austin. She left a
busy household just on the strength of your note.

DR SLOPER (*goes to her, extending his hand*): I am very grateful, ma'am. I should more properly have gone to you, but this is one of my mornings at the Clinic, and I dared not take the time to make a formal call.

MRS MONTGOMERY: I quite understand, Doctor. I am glad to come. I have occasion to know what the Sloper Clinic has meant for the children of this city.

DR SLOPER: Have I seen you there, ma'am?

MRS MONTGOMERY: You saw my oldest girl; she had a very bad croup, and you were wonderful.

DR SLOPER: Well, well, thank you. Mrs Montgomery, will you sit here where we may talk? (*He leads her to a chair.*)

MRS ALMOND: Will you excuse me, Mrs Montgomery? I should like to see my sister while I am here.

MRS MONTGOMERY: Of course, Mrs Almond.

    MRS ALMOND *starts up the stairs.*

DR SLOPER: She's in the kitchen, Liz.

MRS ALMOND: Oh, thank you, Austin!

    MRS ALMOND *goes out.* DR SLOPER *closes the sliding doors. There is a brief silence.*

DR SLOPER: It's difficult to begin, isn't it?

MRS MONTGOMERY: No, Doctor . . .

DR SLOPER: You will have gathered from my note that I wish to ask you a few questions?

MRS MONTGOMERY: Yes, I did.

DR SLOPER: They are about your brother.

MRS MONTGOMERY: Yes, I understood that.

DR SLOPER: Did you tell him that you were coming here this morning.

MRS MONTGOMERY: No, Doctor, I thought I would prefer to tell him *after* I had seen you.

DR SLOPER: Thank you. You must understand my situation, Mrs Montgomery. Your brother wishes to marry my daughter, so I must find out what sort of young man he is.

A good way to do so seemed to be to meet you, which I have proceeded to do.

MRS MONTGOMERY (*politely*): I'm very happy to meet you, Doctor.

DR SLOPER: Mrs Montgomery, if your brother marries my girl, her whole happiness will depend on his being a good fellow. I want you to tell me something about his character. What sort of gentleman is he?

MRS MONTGOMERY: Well, Doctor, he is intelligent and he is charming. He is a wonderful companion.

DR SLOPER: Yes, I know that! But is he reliable? Is he trustworthy? Is he – responsible?

MRS MONTGOMERY: Well, if you mean, is he financially secure, he is not, Doctor. But I'm sure you must know that!

DR SLOPER: Yes, he told me that himself.

MRS MONTGOMERY: That is another thing about Morris. He is honest.

DR SLOPER (*seizing it*): Is he? Is he then honest in his feeling for my daughter?

MRS MONTGOMERY (*gravely*): Oh, I cannot tell you that, Doctor. I never could say what goes on in people's hearts. Could you?

DR SLOPER: I have to try, ma'am. As a doctor I have to try all the time. And now as a father I have to reassure myself that what goes on in your brother's heart will not harm my daughter.

MRS MONTGOMERY: Yes, it is natural to want some assurance. The reason why I came here this morning is that I want that, too. I am very anxious that Morris shall make a happy marriage.

DR SLOPER: Has he always lived with you, ma'am?

MRS MONTGOMERY: Since he was sixteen, Doctor.

DR SLOPER: I have my impression to go by, Mrs Montgomery, but I am in the habit of trusting my impression. Your brother strikes me as selfish.

MRS MONTGOMERY (*calmly*): He is selfish. But then I think we are all rather selfish.

DR SLOPER: He told me that he had used up a small inheritance. Did he handle it well?

MRS MONTGOMERY (*smiling*): Probably you would not think so, Doctor, but from his own point of view he did a great deal with it. He saw Europe, he met many interesting people, he enlarged his capacities.

DR SLOPER: Did he help you, ma'am?

MRS MONTGOMERY: No.

DR SLOPER: Shouldn't he have?

MRS MONTGOMERY: I don't think so.

DR SLOPER: You are a widow; you have children. *I* think so.

MRS MONTGOMERY: You want me to complain about him, sir. But I have no complaint. I have brought him up as if he were my child, and I have accepted the good and the bad in him, just as I accept them in my children.

DR SLOPER: I have made you angry, ma'am. I apologize.

MRS MONTGOMERY: I think, Doctor, you expect too much of people. If you do, you will always be disappointed.

DR SLOPER: You do not disappoint me, Mrs Montgomery.

MRS MONTGOMERY: And Morris has not disappointed *me* —

DR SLOPER (*worriedly*): But you see, these two young people have only known each other two weeks! . . .

MRS MONTGOMERY (*smiles*): Yes, I know. To me, that is a good sign.

DR SLOPER: Is it?

MRS MONTGOMERY: Yes, they are listening only to the promptings of their own two hearts. They have not taken time to consider the consequences or weigh the difficulties. They have just fallen in love.

DR SLOPER: You mean, at first sight?

MRS MONTGOMERY: Why not? That's the way to fall in love, if what you see is pleasing.

DR SLOPER: You know, ma'am, I don't believe in love at first sight.

MRS MONTGOMERY: It's a matter of temperament, Doctor. Morris has always made immediate responses to beauty, in any form.

DR SLOPER: In women?

MRS MONTGOMERY (*smiling*): Oh, yes, indeed! I hope you don't think that's a *bad* thing in a young man, Doctor?

DR SLOPER: No, of course not. I want you to meet my daughter (DR SLOPER *opens sliding doors, walks to staircase and calls up*) Catherine! Catherine!

While DR SLOPER *is in the hall*, MRS MONTGOMERY *looks at the miniature on the table.*

CATHERINE: Yes, Father.

DR SLOPER: Will you come downstairs a moment, please?

MRS MONTGOMERY: I am glad I will meet her. I hoped you would bring us together. (*She picks up the miniature.*) Is this she?

DR SLOPER: No. That is a picture of my wife.

MRS MONTGOMERY: She is very beautiful.

DR SLOPER: Yes, she *was* – very beautiful.

As she is replacing the miniature, CATHERINE *enters the room.*

Catherine, this is Mrs Montgomery, Mr Townsend's sister.

MRS MONTGOMERY: Ah, Miss Sloper! — (*She holds out her hand.*)

CATHERINE (*very shy*): How do you do?

MRS MONTGOMERY: I am very happy to meet you.

CATHERINE: Thank you. (*To Dr Sloper.*) Didn't Morris come?

DR SLOPER: No, Catherine.

CATHERINE (*desperately anxious*): Isn't he coming?

DR SLOPER (*patiently*): His appointment is for eleven, Catherine.

CATHERINE (*stealing a look at the clock*): Oh ... yes. (*Turns back to Mrs Montgomery, and with great effort*): Are your children well?

MRS MONTGOMERY: Quite well, thank you. I hope Morris will bring you to see me and my family very soon.

CATHERINE (*halting*): Yes.

MRS MONTGOMERY (*they look at each other.* MRS MONTGOMERY *sees that she must start it*): Er . . . your aunt tells me that you are interested in the hospital charities?

CATHERINE (*diffident*): Yes, I am.

MRS MONTGOMERY: As a doctor's daughter you must be very useful there.

CATHERINE: I hope so. (*Pause.*)

MRS MONTGOMERY: My brother tells me that you have an aunt visiting you, Miss Sloper?

CATHERINE: Yes. My Aunt Penniman.

MRS MONTGOMERY: It is delightful to have people to whom one can show New York. Does she like our city?

CATHERINE: Yes.

DR SLOPER: Catherine, perhaps you will offer Mrs Montgomery a glass of the Madeira?

CATHERINE (*rising instantly*): Yes, indeed. Please excuse me. (*Half-way to the door she turns.*) Father, may I ask Mrs Montgomery to try my coriander cookies . . .?

DR SLOPER: Very well.

MRS MONTGOMERY: I should like to very much, Miss Sloper.

CATHERINE: I think you will find them quite delicate. (*She goes out.*)

MRS MONTGOMERY (*after a pause*): She is very shy.

DR SLOPER: Yes, she is.

MRS MONTGOMERY: Perhaps she is less shy with Morris?

DR SLOPER: Has your brother listened *only* to the promptings of his heart?

MRS MONTGOMERY: I cannot tell you that, Doctor.

DR SLOPER: You said, love at first sight. Well, you were right about Catherine. Were you right about your brother?

MRS MONTGOMERY: Well, I – I can only suppose that Morris is more mature in his feelings than I had thought. This time he has not sought out superficial charms, but has considered the gentle character underneath.

DR SLOPER: Are you being honest, ma'am?

MRS MONTGOMERY: I think I am.

DR SLOPER: Well, I think that her money is the prime attraction.

MRS MONTGOMERY: What money?

DR SLOPER: She is an heiress! Didn't your brother tell you that?

MRS MONTGOMERY: No . . . he did not.

DR SLOPER: She has ten thousand dollars a year from her mother, and on my death she will have twice as much more.

MRS MONTGOMERY: She will be immensely rich!

DR SLOPER: Yes, she will. Of course, if she marries a man I don't approve, I shall leave my part to the Clinic.

MRS MONTGOMERY (slowly): But she has the ten now?

DR SLOPER: Yes.

MRS MONTGOMERY: That is still a great deal of money, Doctor.

DR SLOPER: It is. And consider how he has behaved with money. He gratified his every wish! But did he help you with the children? No! He enlarged his capacities in Europe! (He picks up the chamois gloves.) He left his gloves here yesterday. Look at them . . . the finest chamois. Look at yours . . .

MRS MONTGOMERY looks at the gloves. There is a pause.

MRS MONTGOMERY: I don't know, Doctor, I don't.

DR SLOPER: Will he help you with this fortune he hopes to marry? I would stake my life that he would not. Yet he has a natural tie to you. . . a true affection.

MRS MONTGOMERY: You must follow your own dictates, Doctor.

DR SLOPER (*he tosses the gloves on the centre table*): Tell me she is not a victim of his avariciousness – tell me I'm wrong.

MRS MONTGOMERY: I must go now.

DR SLOPER: Mrs Montgomery, she will believe you. Will you tell my daughter the truth about your brother's motives?

MRS MONTGOMERY: I don't know the truth, Doctor. I don't know the truth of anyone's motives.

DR SLOPER: I think his are clear . . . pitifully clear. He is in love with her money.

MRS MONTGOMERY: You want me to tell her *that?*

DR SLOPER: Yes.

MRS MONTGOMERY: I won't!

DR SLOPER: You see, you still protect him!

MRS MONTGOMERY: No, it is the girl I protect! Am I to tell her that she is undesirable – that she is unloved! Why, it would break her heart! I would not say that to any girl!

DR SLOPER (*after a pause*): Mrs Montgomery, what am I to do?

MRS MONTGOMERY (*near door*): I don't know. (*Then deliberately.*) But if you are so opposed to this marriage, then as a father you must find a kinder way of stopping it. Good day, Doctor.

DR SLOPER: Good day, Mrs. Montgomery. (*She goes.*)
   As DR SLOPER *closes the door behind her and walks back into the drawing-room,* MRS ALMOND *and* MRS PENNIMAN, *dressed for shopping, enter from the back of the house.*

MRS ALMOND: Oh, was that Mrs Montgomery leaving? I wanted Lavinia to meet her.

DR SLOPER: Yes, Liz, she left.

MRS PENNIMAN: Did you like her, Austin?

DR SLOPER: Very much.

MRS PENNIMAN: Good! Catherine has just asked Elizabeth if Marian might be her maid-of-honour!

DR SLOPER: She must get over it. He is worthless.

MRS PENNIMAN (*shocked*): What!

MRS ALMOND: You will not make Catherine see that.

DR SLOPER: I will present her with a pair of spectacles.

MRS PENNIMAN: Austin, her entire happiness lies in your hands!

DR SLOPER: That's right, Lavinia.

MRS PENNIMAN: You will kill her if you deny her this marriage!

DR SLOPER: Nonsense!

MRS PENNIMAN: You will! She is in a pitiable state of anxiety. She passed a dreadful night!

DR SLOPER: My dear, people don't die of one dreadful night, or even of a dozen. Remember, I'm a physician.

MRS PENNIMAN: Your being one has not prevented you from already losing one member of your family.

DR SLOPER (*pointed*): It may not prevent me, either, from losing the society of another!

MRS PENNIMAN: Oh!

MRS ALMOND: Austin, have you forgotten what it's like to love someone?

DR SLOPER: I hope not.

MRS ALMOND: Then have compassion on Catherine.

DR SLOPER (*he paces the room*): I can't. She has lacked discrimination; she has been taken in! She must not love people who don't deserve to be loved. I don't.

MRS PENNIMAN: Your power to love has withered away.

DR SLOPER: My judgement hasn't! The man's a fortune hunter!

MRS ALMOND: I don't know, Austin . . . in these things one can never be sure.

DR SLOPER: Oh, Liz, be sensible! He has walked in here as if this were a shooting-box, and Catherine and I were the pigeons!

MRS ALMOND: But you have said yourself that she is not a girl likely to attract many men. And if this man likes her, wants to marry her, and will take good care of her, and her money, what is lost?

DR SLOPER (*he stands still now*): What assurance have I that he would take good care of her? The contrary is more likely. He has a devoted sister to whom he owes everything; he has never made the smallest attempt to take care of her!

MRS PENNIMAN (*wretchedly*): You have only *her* word for that!

MRS ALMOND (*sees* CATHERINE *coming*): Ssh!

　　CATHERINE *enters carrying a small silver tray.*

DR SLOPER: Mrs Montgomery has left, Catherine.

CATHERINE (*surprised, stands still with the tray*): Oh, I took too long. I wanted to make the tray particularly nice.

DR SLOPER: It was not your fault, my dear. We had concluded our talk.

CATHERINE (*putting the tray down*): Concluded . . .?

DR SLOPER: Yes.

CATHERINE: Did Mrs Montgomery tell you something bad, Father?

DR SLOPER: No, Catherine.

CATHERINE: I did not impress her favourably, did I?

DR SLOPER: Good heavens, child, don't hold yourself so cheaply!

　　The clock on the mantelpiece starts to strike eleven.

CATHERINE: I was embarrassed. I won't be another time. (*As the last stroke is heard, the front doorbell sounds.*) That will be Mr Townsend.

DR SLOPER: You had better go to your room, Catherine.

CATHERINE: Yes. (*She turns before she goes out, and speaks with great effort.*) Father, tell him . . . tell him about me. You know me so well . . . It will not be immodest in you to . . . to praise me a little. (*She goes out.*)

MRS ALMOND (*touched*): What are you going to do?

DR SLOPER: What *can* I do? How is it possible to protect such a willing victim?

MRS ALMOND: Austin, You could take her to Europe with you.

MRS PENNIMAN: Oh, no!

DR SLOPER: I ... I had hopes of going alone.

MRS ALMOND: I know that. But this is no time for reliving your memories. A European trip might be just the thing for Catherine. (MARIA *comes into the hall.* MRS ALMOND *rises.*)

> MRS PENNIMAN *rises.* MARIA *has been waiting for instructions.*

DR SLOPER: See who it is, Maria.

MARIA: Yes, sir. (*She goes to the door and admits* MORRIS TOWNSEND, *off-stage.*)

MRS ALMOND: We will go, Lavinia.

MARIA (*off-stage*): Good morning, Mr Townsend.

MORRIS (*off-stage*): Good morning. Is Dr Sloper at home?

MARIA (*off-stage*): Yes, sir.

> MORRIS *enters. He smiles as he sees the women.*

MORRIS: What a pleasant surprise! Good morning, Mrs Almond, Mrs Penniman – Doctor.

MRS ALMOND: Good morning.

MRS PENNIMAN: Good morning.

DR SLOPER: How do you do, Mr Townsend.

MRS ALMOND: Mrs Penniman and I are just leaving.

MORRIS: Oh, I'm sorry.

MRS PENNIMAN: On our way to market ... It's such a beautiful morning, we thought —

MRS ALMOND (*firmly*): Come, Lavinia, we must be on our way. Good day, Austin. Good-bye, Mr Townsend. (*She goes out.*)

MRS PENNIMAN (*stops in front of Morris on her way to the hall*): Mr Townsend ... I ...

DR SLOPER (*interrupting*): Good day, Lavinia.

MRS PENNIMAN (*to* MORRIS): I – I hope you have a pleasant visit. (*She bows.*)

MORRIS (*smiling*): Thank you. I hope *you* have as pleasant
   marketing . . .

DR SLOPER (*dryly*): Good-bye, Lavinia.

   MRS PENNIMAN *is about to speak again.*

MRS ALMOND: Lavinia.

MORRIS: You expected me, sir?

DR SLOPER: Yes, I did. (*He looks at the mantel clock.*) You are
   admirably prompt.

MORRIS (*smiling*): I deserve no credit for that, Doctor. I could
   hardly be late for so important an occasion as this one.

DR SLOPER: Yes . . . Catherine told me what has been going
   on between you. Will you sit there? (*He indicates the sofa.*)

MORRIS: Thank you. (*As he sits.*) I have been walking all
   morning, and you know, sir, I find New York as lovely
   as any city in Europe at this time of year.

DR SLOPER: Yes. You must allow me to say, Mr Townsend,
   that it would have been becoming of you to give me notice
   of your intentions before they had gone so far.

MORRIS: I should have done so, Doctor, if you had not let
   your daughter so much liberty. She seems to me quite her
   own mistress.

DR SLOPER: She is. But she is not, I trust, quite so emanci-
   pated as to choose a husband without consulting me. The
   truth is, your little affair has come to a head faster than I
   expected. It was only the other day Catherine made your
   acquaintance. (DR SLOPER *sits opposite Morris.*)

MORRIS: We have not been slow to arrive at understanding.
   My interest in Miss Sloper began the first time I saw her.

DR SLOPER: Did it not even precede your first meeting?

MORRIS (*looks at him an instant*): I certainly had already heard
   that she was a charming girl.

DR SLOPER: A charming girl – that's what you think her?

MORRIS (*smiling*): Otherwise I should not be sitting here.

DR SLOPER: My dear young man, you must be very suscept-
   ible. As Catherine's father, I have, I hope, a just appreciation

of her many good qualities. But I don't mind telling you that I've never quite thought of her in that light.

MORRIS (*smiles politely*): I don't know what I might think of her if I were her father. I can't put myself in that place. I speak from my own point of view.

DR SLOPER: You speak very well ... but did you really expect that I would throw my daughter into your arms?

MORRIS: No, I had an idea you didn't like me.

DR SLOPER: What gave you that idea?

MORRIS: The fact that I'm poor.

DR SLOPER: That has a harsh sound, but it's about the truth. You have no means, profession, visible resources or prospects, and so you're in a category from which *not* to choose a son-in-law. Particularly not for my daughter, who is a weak young woman with a large fortune.

MORRIS: I don't think Miss Sloper is a weak woman.

DR SLOPER: Mr Townsend, I've known my daughter all her life: you have known her only two weeks. Besides, even if she were not weak, you still are penniless.

MORRIS: Ah, yes! *That is my weakness!* And therefore, you mean, I am mercenary. I only want your daughter's money!

DR SLOPER: No, I don't say that – *You* say that! I say simply you are in the wrong category.

MORRIS: But your daughter doesn't marry a category! She marries a man – a man whom she is good enough to say she loves!

DR SLOPER: A man who offers nothing in return.

MORRIS: Is it possible to offer more than the most tender affection and a life-long devotion?

DR SLOPER: A life-long devotion is measured *after* the fact. Meanwhile it is usual to give a few material securities. What are yours? A handsome face and figure and a very good manner.

MORRIS: But really, Doctor, I ...

DR SLOPER: Oh, they're excellent as far as they go, but they don't go far enough.

MORRIS: There is one thing you should add to them – the word of a gentleman.

DR SLOPER (*ironically*): The word of a gentleman that you will always love Catherine? You must be a fine gentleman to be sure of that.

MORRIS: The word of a gentleman that I am not mercenary! I care no more for your daughter's fortune than for the ashes in that grate!

DR SLOPER: I take note – I take note. But even with that solemn vow, you are still in the category of which I spoke.

MORRIS (*trying to regain ground*): You think I am an idler?

DR SLOPER: It doesn't matter what I think, once I tell you I just don't think of you as a son-in-law.

MORRIS: You think I'd squander her money!

DR SLOPER: I plead guilty to *that*.

MORRIS: That's because I spent my own, I suppose? Well, it was just because it *was* my own that I spent it! And I have made no debts. When it was gone I stopped. I don't owe a penny in the world.

DR SLOPER: Allow me to ask, what are you living on now?

MORRIS: The remnants of my property.

DR SLOPER: Thank you. By the way, you left your gloves here yesterday. (*Hands gloves.*)

MORRIS (*pleading now*): Thank you. Dr Sloper, don't you care to gratify your daughter? Do you enjoy the idea of making her miserable?

DR SLOPER: I'm resigned to her thinking me a tyrant for a few months.

MORRIS: For a few months!

DR SLOPER: For a lifetime, then. She may as well be miserable that way, as with you.

MORRIS: Ah, you are not polite, sir!

DR SLOPER: You press me to it; you argue too much.

MORRIS: Dr Sloper, I have fallen in love with your daughter. I am not the kind of man you would choose for her . . . and for good reasons. I have committed every folly, every indiscretion a young man can find to commit . . . I have squandered an inheritance . . . I have gambled . . . I have drunk unwisely . . . I admit, I confess all these things . . .

DR SLOPER: Mr Townsend, I am acting in the capacity of a judge, not your confessor!

MORRIS: I tell you these things myself, Doctor, because I love Catherine, and I have a great deal at stake.

DR SLOPER: Then you have lost it.

MORRIS: No, sir.

DR SLOPER: Just as surely as if you placed your pittance on the losing number . . . It is over. You have lost.

MORRIS: Don't be too sure of that, sir. I believe I have only to say the word and she will walk out of this house and follow me.

DR SLOPER: You are impertinent!

MORRIS: And may I add, Dr Sloper, if I did not love your daughter as much as I do, I should not have put up with the indignities you have offered me today.

DR SLOPER: You have only to leave my house to escape them. Good day, Mr Townsend.

MORRIS: Good day, sir.

    MORRIS *has put on his hat, and turns to the door. Before he reaches it to open it and leave,* CATHERINE *calls from the top of the stairs.*

CATHERINE (*unseen*): Wait, Morris, wait! (*She runs down the stairs and goes to Morris.*)

DR SLOPER: *Catherine!*

CATHERINE: You promised me, Morris, you promised you would be respectful when you saw my father!

DR SLOPER: *Catherine!*

CATHERINE (*taking Morris by the arm and leading him back to the drawing-room, enters*): What is the matter, Father?

DR SLOPER: Catherine, you are without dignity!

CATHERINE: I don't care. Why are you angry? Why are you and Morris quarrelling?

DR SLOPER: Catherine, you must give him up.

CATHERINE: Give him up? Why? What has he done? What did Mrs Montgomery tell you.

MORRIS: My sister? Have you spoken with her?

DR SLOPER: She paid me a visit this morning . . . on my invitation.

CATHERINE: Father, you must see how painful this is for me. Surely you will want me to know your reasons?

DR SLOPER: He is a selfish idler.

MORRIS: My sister never told you that.

CATHERINE: But, Father, I know he loves me.

DR SLOPER: I know he does not!

CATHERINE: In God's name, Father, tell me what makes you so sure!

DR SLOPER (*a pause*): My poor child, I can't tell you that – you must simply take my word for it.

CATHERINE: Father, I can't! I can't! I love him! (*Despairing.*) I have promised to marry him, to stay by him, no matter what comes.

DR SLOPER: So he forearmed himself by getting a promise like that, did he? (*To Morris.*) You are beneath contempt!

CATHERINE (*stolidly*): Don't abuse him, Father! (*After a pause.*) I think we shall marry quite soon.

DR SLOPER (*turns away – starts for his study*): Then it is no further concern of mine.

CATHERINE: I'm sorry.

MORRIS: Dr Sloper! (DR SLOPER *stops and turns to him.*) Dr Sloper, as much as I love Catherine, we cannot marry without your approval. It would bring unhappiness to all of us.

DR SLOPER: Do you mean that, sir?

MORRIS: Yes.

DR SLOPER: Mr Townsend, I am going to Europe for six months. I would like Catherine to go with me.

CATHERINE: *Europe?*

DR SLOPER: I would like you very much to go, Catherine.

CATHERINE: Why?

MORRIS: Your father thinks you will forget me, Catherine.

CATHERINE: I don't want to go!

DR SLOPER: Are you afraid? Are you afraid of a separation?

CATHERINE: I shall still love him when I come back.

DR SLOPER: You are romantic, my dear, and very inexperienced.

CATHERINE: Yes, I am.

DR SLOPER: And at the moment you are exalted with the feeling of undying devotion to a lover. You are very sure of your love . . . But, Catherine, do you dare to test him?

CATHERINE: You underestimate him.

DR SLOPER: I don't think so. (*Then looks squarely at Morris.*)

MORRIS (*after a pause, goes to Catherine and takes her hand*): Catherine, go to Europe. (*Now he looks squarely at Dr Sloper.*) Go to Europe with your father.

CURTAIN

ACT TWO

SCENE ONE

It is an April night six months later. There is a cosy glow from the fireplace. MRS PENNIMAN *and* MORRIS *are sitting at a backgammon table.* MRS PENNIMAN *is shaking the dice box.* MORRIS *is watching her as he sips a glass of brandy.* MRS PENNIMAN *throws the dice.* MORRIS *leans across the table to see the count.*

MRS PENNIMAN: Now this young couple I was telling you about —

MORRIS: Well, well, that's just the number you wanted.

MRS PENNIMAN: Why, so it is! (*She moves a checker.*)

MORRIS: Ah, ah, you can't move *that* one!

MRS PENNIMAN: Oh, no, that's right. You have me blocked, haven't you?

MORRIS: Yes . . .

MRS PENNIMAN: Well, now, let me see . . . Which one shall I move, Morris?

MORRIS (*smiles and points*): That one.

MRS PENNIMAN (*studies the move, then laughs*): Oh, no, no, indeed! I'll do nothing of the sort! That's why you always win! (MORRIS *laughs.*) And this is the night we must settle, isn't it? (*She laughs.*)

MORRIS (*holds up the brandy*): No, No, please. Let your hospitality be full payment. (*He refills his glass and leans over to do the same for hers.*) May I?

MRS PENNIMAN: No, thank you, Morris.

MORRIS: By the way, what will you say when the Doctor asks where his brandy has gone to?

MRS PENNIMAN (*laughing*): I shall say it was a cold winter and *I* drank it.

MORRIS: You're right about the cold winter – a lonely· one, too. (*Quickly gallant.*) Were it not for your kindness, it would have been unbearable.

MRS PENNIMAN: Oh . . . Thank you, Morris. (MORRIS *picks up dice box, shakes it.*) Now, this young couple I was telling you about – Well, they came to the Rectory long after supper-time, and the Reverend Penniman . . . I miss him so . . . performed the ceremony without a moment's hesitation . . . (*With romantic remembrance.*) I was one of the witnesses . . . The Reverend's assistant, a nice young man, was the other, and do you know, we heard later that the father was reconciled to the young man, and thought the world of him.

MORRIS: And you think the Doctor will be reconciled, too?

MRS PENNIMAN: I'm sure of it. May I see that letter again?

MORRIS (*getting letter out of his pocket*): But when I let her go off with him, I thought we would have his consent by now. (*Hands the letter to her.*)

MRS PENNIMAN (*reading*): 'February the 14th' . . . ummh . . . almost a month and a half ago. Well, maybe since she wrote that he has given his consent. (*Hands it back.*)

MORRIS: Maybe. But I cannot take the chance. (*Indicates the place in the letter.*) You see, she says here — (*Reads.*) 'I dare not mention your name to Father. He has not been well, and I fear to anger him.'

MRS PENNIMAN: You see, she still loves you, Morris.

MORRIS: Yes. (*Takes the letter and puts it back in his pocket.*)

MRS PENNIMAN: Then you have nothing to worry about.

MORRIS: No . . . if she will really run off with me, I think we can make things come right.

MRS PENNIMAN (*laughs*): I've never kept a secret this long in my entire life.

MORRIS: You must keep it a little while longer, Mrs Penniman. (*Looks at the mantel clock.*) My gracious, it's almost nine-thirty. That's the latest we've played all winter.

MRS PENNIMAN: The time passes so quickly.

MORRIS: It does, indeed.

MRS PENNIMAN: Can I offer you a tidbit – a sandwich?

MORRIS (*rises*): No, thank you. I am still savouring that excellent dinner.

MRS PENNIMAN: Oh, wouldn't you like to smoke?

MORRIS: May I?

MRS PENNIMAN: Pray do.

MORRIS (*selects a cigar from Dr Sloper's humidor. He takes the band off and tosses it into the fireplace*): Mrs Penniman, you will have to tell Catherine all the details tomorrow. The moment you are alone with her, as soon after the boat docks as possible, you must tell her everything about our plans. And it would be well if she did not unpack.

MRS PENNIMAN: Morris, I shall be at the slip at ten o'clock tomorrow morning.

MORRIS: Ten o'clock? What if the ship docks earlier?

MRS PENNIMAN: Then I'll be there at seven – at break of day, if it makes you less nervous.

MORRIS: I wish I could have written about this to Catherine . . .

MRS PENNIMAN (*reassuring*): I shall tell her all the details the moment I see her.

MORRIS: Yes . . . but planning an elopement by messenger, it's rather cold.

MRS PENNIMAN (*smiling*): It will be the happiest news she has ever heard! Leave it to me. Morris, I wish I could go with you both tomorrow night . . .?

MORRIS: You must stay behind to pacify the Doctor.

MRS PENNIMAN: Yes, I know – but I would so enjoy it! Think of it; a private marriage! In the dead of night! Catherine is a lucky girl!

MORRIS (*thoughtfully*): I hope we shall both be lucky.

MRS PENNIMAN: Of course you will be! Austin will be furious.

MORRIS: What?

MRS PENNIMAN: Oh, for a few weeks, or a few months, but then he will come round.

MORRIS (*unpleasantly reminded*): He told my sister he'd disinherit Catherine. Do you think that's possible?

MRS PENNIMAN: That was a threat, Morris, and a very foolish one. He can't take away the ten thousand dollars a year Catherine already has.

MORRIS (*musingly*): That would be small comfort.

MRS PENNIMAN (*surprised*): Ten thousand dollars ... small ...?

MORRIS: On ten, ma'am, you live like your neighbour. Even Arthur and Marian will have ten. But thirty is something to look forward to. On thirty you live — (*His hand takes in the room.*) like this.

MRS PENNIMAN: You like this house, don't you, Morris?

MORRIS: Yes, ma'am, I do. From the first evening that I was brought here, I have admired it, and all the things in it. The Doctor is a man of fine taste. It is strange that although we do not like each other, we seem to like the same things.

MRS PENNIMAN: You are more appreciative than Austin, Morris. Even in the way you have understood Catherine, and responded to her true worth.

MORRIS: Yes, Catherine ... (*He handles the wine glass.*) But also other things. For instance, this crystal – it's Venetian. Do you know when I was in Venice, although I was down to my last fifty dollars, I bought two pieces of Venetian glass and kept them for a few weeks just to have them and look at them? Then I was really poor and had to sell them in order to leave. I love such things ... I always have.

MRS PENNIMAN: It will be a bond between you when Austin has at last forgiven you.

MORRIS: I hope so. But I am afraid that he will have contempt for my fine tastes.

MRS PENNIMAN: Why should he, since he shares them?

The sound of a carriage passing in the street is heard.

MORRIS (*holding the glass*): He has earned this by his work. He believes that every man should do the same. The trouble is that some of us cannot. (*The carriage stops* — MORRIS *takes notice.*) What *is* that outside? It sounds like a coach – What *is* that outside?

We hear the carriage door close – and voices.

MRS PENNIMAN: Have we callers?

MORRIS: You had better look out of the window.

MRS PENNIMAN *does so.*

MRS PENNIMAN: Good heavens, they are here!

MORRIS: *They are!* (*Trapped, he starts for the hall.*)

MRS PENNIMAN: Morris, don't go! The brandy! (*She quickly folds the backgammon board;* MORRIS *snatches his cigar from the ashtray and runs towards the hall. As he is about to turn towards the back of the house,* MRS PENNIMAN *stops him.*)

MORRIS: Where shall I put it?

MRS PENNIMAN: Go downstairs and wait in the kitchen – Morris! Your hat!

He takes his hat from the hall table as MARIA *hurries forward to open the front door.*

MORRIS (*to Mrs Penniman*): Tell her everything!

MRS PENNIMAN (*rushing him towards the kitchen*): I will.

MORRIS: Tell her I love her!

MRS PENNIMAN: I will, I will!

MORRIS *goes out.*

MARIA (*rushing to the door*): I think it's them, ma'am. (*Off-stage.*) Doctor and Miss Catherine, you are really back!

CATHERINE (*off-stage*): Yes, Maria, sooner than we thought. (*Enters.*) Dear Aunt Lavinia!

MRS PENNIMAN: Oh, Catherine, I am so glad to see you!

(CATHERINE *and* MRS PENNIMAN *embrace*.) Why, you are so smart! You look so French, my dear!

CATHERINE: Yes, it's new. Have you been well, Aunt?

MRS PENNIMAN: Very well!

CATHERINE: Tell me quickly, how is Morris?

MRS PENNIMAN (*smiling*): The last time I saw him he was very well . . .

DR SLOPER (*off-stage*): See that they carry those boxes around to the back, Maria.

MRS PENNIMAN: But he told me to tell you . . .

CATHERINE (*quickly as she hears* DR SLOPER *enter*): Shhh . . .

MRS PENNIMAN (*embracing Dr Sloper*): Austin, welcome home. But we never expected you!

DR SLOPER: You mean never again, Lavinia?

MRS PENNIMAN: I was going to meet you tomorrow with the carriage . . .

MARIA (*crossing the hall*): I will open the back door for them, sir. (*Goes out.*)

CATHERINE: Oh, it is so good to be home! Isn't it, Father?

MRS PENNIMAN: Were you lonely, Cathie?

CATHERINE: Yes, Aunt Lavinia, I was.

MRS PENNIMAN: Of course you were! No matter how magnificent distant places are, there is always someone at home one misses. Isn't that so? (*Turns to Dr Sloper.*) Where are you going, Austin?

DR SLOPER: I have a beastly cold, Lavinia. I want some hot water.

MRS PENNIMAN (*quickly blocking him*): I'll get it.

DR SLOPER: I want some brandy, too.

MRS PENNIMAN: There's some there . . . there in the decanter.

DR SLOPER: Is there? Well! Have you taken to drink, Lavinia?

MRS PENNIMAN: Yes, a little, for my heart. I'll tell Maria about the hot water.

Goes out. DR SLOPER *removes his cape, then winds clock at mantel.*

CATHERINE (*timidly*): I am very glad you decided to leave the ship tonight, Father. (*No answer.*) You must be as glad to be home as I. (*No answer.*) I know you have not felt well these last days. I wish you had let me try to take care of you a little. (*No answer.*) Sometimes I almost felt that you did not want me by you . . . (DR SLOPER's *back is turned.*) It is distressing to be ill away from home. You will be content now that we are back . . .

MRS PENNIMAN (*re-entering*): Maria will be right in. Now tell me everything. I don't care how tired you are. I want to hear everything you did.

DR SLOPER *picks up cigar band from the hearth.*

CATHERINE (*smiling*): Dear Aunt Lavinia, that would take a year.

MRS PENNIMAN: What did you like most?

CATHERINE: Well, we saw so much.

MRS PENNIMAN: You loved Paris! Of course you did. It's a woman's city, isn't it? But you liked it too, didn't you, Austin?

DR SLOPER: Is she bringing that hot water?

MRS PENNIMAN: Yes, yes, right away.

DR SLOPER: Well!

MRS PENNIMAN: Well I don't suppose you want to hear what I did all winter. The fact is, I did nothing – nothing at all.

DR SLOPER: Your heart would improve, Lavinia, if you gave up smoking cigars.

MRS PENNIMAN: What?

MARIA *enters with small pitcher of hot water and a toddy glass.*

MARIA: Here you are, Doctor. (*He sits down wearily.*) I can't tell you how glad I am you and Miss Catherine are home, sir. (DR SLOPER *acknowledges this with a bow.*)

We didn't expect you until tomorrow, so the bedrooms are cold. But it will only take a jiffy to lay fires. They'll be warm in an instant. (*She goes out with the hats and coats.*)

DR SLOPER: Thank you, Maria. Well, Lavinia, do you prefer my Massachusetts Home Grown or my Sumatras?

MRS PENNIMAN: I don't know what you are talking about, Austin.

DR SLOPER: When I detect the delicious aroma of bay rum – see my brandy decanter half-empty, and find loose cigar bands in my grate, I can only think of one person. What has happened to Mr Townsend? Has he jumped out of the window?

MRS PENNIMAN: That's right; he did stop by to inquire about you.

CATHERINE: This evening, Aunt? Has he been here this evening?

MRS PENNIMAN (*embarrassed*): Yes, he just happened to be in the neighbourhood and stopped by for an instant. (*To Dr Sloper.*) I have hardly seen him all winter. He had been most circumspect.

DR SLOPER: Really, I should have expected him to make this house his club. It is such a comfortable place to rest in while other people are working.

MRS PENNIMAN (*nervously*): Catherine, dear, I know I shouldn't ask, but did you bring me anything?

CATHERINE (*watching Dr Sloper*): Yes, Aunt. A cashmere shawl.

MRS PENNIMAN: Oh, just what I asked for! Do come and show it to me, dear.

CATHERINE: It's in my bag. Maria will unpack it for you.

MRS PENNIMAN (*escaping*): You will come later, won't you? (*Goes out.*)

CATHERINE: Father, I hardly expected you would speak that

way of Morris after all this time . . . Particularly since we have done everything you asked us to do.

DR SLOPER: What a ridiculous position to be in! Well, it's a fitting ending to the most futile six months of my life.

CATHERINE: They were not futile to me. I thought they were wonderful.

DR SLOPER: Wonderful! Yes, that's the very word you used, Catherine. Tintoretto was a wonderful painter; the ices at the Café Riche were wonderful; almost as wonderful as Michael Angelo's David.

CATHERINE: If you mean I did not appreciate it, you are wrong. I appreciated everything.

DR SLOPER: You saw *nothing*, Catherine! What was Rome and all its glories to you? Just a place where you might receive a letter from him!

CATHERINE: This is why you have not let me approach you all these weeks, because I told you I still loved him . . .

DR SLOPER: You carried the image of that wastrel with you every place we went. He blotted out any pleasure we might have had . . . I waited a long time for my trip to Paris. I never thought I should see it all arm in arm with him. (*Disgusted.*) Well, there are some things one cannot teach people, even one's own daughter! One cannot give her eyes or understanding if she has none.

CATHERINE: But I have eyes, and I have understanding, Father. You were not thinking of me in Paris . . . you were with my mother.

DR SLOPER: I wish I had been! (*There is a pause.*)

CATHERINE: I see our trip has not changed you.

DR SLOPER: Nor you . . . nor Townsend. Well, I suppose you'll be going off with him any time now?

CATHERINE: Yes, if he will have me.

DR SLOPER (*sipping his drink*): Have you! (*Laughs.*) Oh, really, Catherine! He ought to be very grateful to me; I've done a mighty good thing for him in taking you abroad. (*His ironic inflection increases.*) Six months ago you were perhaps a little limited ... a little rustic; but now you should be a most entertaining companion!

CATHERINE: I will try to be.

DR SLOPER: You will have to be very witty indeed, my dear girl! Your gaiety and brilliance will have to make up the difference between the ten thousand dollars a year he'll have and the thirty thousand he expects.

CATHERINE: He doesn't love me for that.

DR SLOPER (*slowly and with contempt*): No? What else, then, Catherine? Your beauty? Your grace, your charm? Your quick tongue and subtle wit?

CATHERINE: He admires me ...

DR SLOPER: Catherine, I've been patient with you. I've tried not to be unkind, but now it is time for you to realize the truth. How many women and girls do you think he might have had in this town.

CATHERINE: He finds me – pleasing ...

DR SLOPER: Yes, I'm sure he does. A hundred women are prettier, and a thousand more clever, but you have one virtue that outshines them all!

CATHERINE (*fearfully*): What – what is that, Father?

DR SLOPER: Your money.

CATHERINE (*slumps into a chair and puts her face in her hands*): Oh, Father! What a monstrous thing to say to me ...!

DR SLOPER: I don't expect you to believe that. I've known you all your life and have yet to see you learn anything. (*He rises and sees her embroidery frame.*) With one exception, my dear ... you embroider neatly. (*He picks up his glass.*) Well, since I shan't be at the wedding, I'll drink your health up in my bed. (*He bows.*) Good night, daughter mine! (*He goes up the stairs.*)

CATHERINE, *crushed, remains seated, her head bowed.* MRS PENNIMAN *comes into the hall, pauses at the foot of the stairs, makes sure that Dr Sloper has gone into his room, then enters the parlour furtively.*

MRS PENNIMAN (*whispering*): Catherine, I've got a surprise for you! (CATHERINE *takes no notice.*) What would you like most in the world?

CATHERINE (*aware now that* MRS PENNIMAN *is in the room*): Aunt Penniman, does Morris still love me?

    MRS PENNIMAN *laughs. She tiptoes into the hall. She beckons Morris to come forward and to do it quietly.* MORRIS *tiptoes into the parlour.* CATHERINE *does not see him. He stands behind her and calls her softly.*

MORRIS: Catherine . . .

CATHERINE (*hearing his voice as in a dream, turns – after a moment she realizes that this is true*): Morris!

MORRIS: Yes, it is your Morris, who has waited for you for six months.

    He takes her hand. MRS PENNIMAN, *pleased with her intrigue, softly closes the parlour doors and leaves them alone.*

CATHERINE: Morris, oh Morris . . . I'm so pleased to see you!

MORRIS: I could not wait another night through. Have you been true to me, Catherine? Have you been constant and faithful?

CATHERINE: Oh, yes!

MORRIS: You have not forgotten me? You have not changed your mind?

CATHERINE: No, no.

MORRIS: I was afraid you might have! I was full of doubts and fears. That's why I could not go home without seeing you. We didn't expect you until tomorrow. I was sitting there when your father knocked on his front door.

CATHERINE (*she looks at him adoringly*): You haven't changed, Morris. You are the same as ever.

    He draws her into his arms – they embrace.

MORRIS: Has your Aunt told you about my plan?

CATHERINE: Your plan?

MORRIS: For our marriage? . . . our elopement?

CATHERINE (*bewildered*): Our elopement —?

MORRIS: It is for tomorrow night! At a country parsonage, up on Murray's Hill. There is a Reverend Lispenard there who knows our story and is prepared to help us. (CATHERINE *stands transfixed and speechless.*) *Catherine, do hear me?*

CATHERINE: Oh, I love you so! (*She throws her arms around him and they embrace.*) Tell me what to do.

MORRIS: I have a closed carriage engaged. I will come to the corner of the Square at five in the afternoon, before the Doctor comes back from his calls. We will load your trunks, and drive to the parsonage. After the marriage, we will spend the night at an inn up the river. And the next day we will go to Albany on our honeymoon.

CATHERINE (*in heaven*): My husband!

MORRIS: Do you like my plan?

CATHERINE: I think its wonderful! I've brought you such a beautiful silk waistcoat. I will unpack it and you must wear it for our wedding.

MORRIS (*pleased*): My dear girl.

CATHERINE (*shyly*): And I bought you a set of buttons at Barrere's in Paris.

MORRIS: Buttons?

CATHERINE: They are rubies and pearls . . . they are quite nice.

MORRIS (*delighted*): My dear, dear girl! (*He embraces her.*) How happy we shall be!

CATHERINE (*disturbed for a moment*): Morris, my father caught cold on the voyage. What if he should not go out on his calls tomorrow?

MORRIS: Well, then, we must wait until the day after.

CATHERINE: No, I cannot stay here any longer. I couldn't bear it!

MORRIS: But it's only one more day!

CATHERINE: No, Morris, I cannot stay! You don't know how it is with me. (*She has an inspiration.*) Morris, take me tonight!

MORRIS: Tonight! How can we?

CATHERINE: We must! My cases and bags are all downstairs. In another hour everyone will be asleep. We can slip away quietly; no one will hear us! Morris, I beg you! I implore you! If you love me, take me away tonight . . .

MORRIS: But where would we go?

CATHERINE: To your sister's – or to the Reverend Lispenard. It won't matter to him that we are one day sooner. And it matters so terribly to me!

MORRIS (*makes up his mind*): Very well! . . . we'll do it. (*He looks at the little clock on the mantel.*) It is almost ten-thirty. I will leave and find a carriage. I can be back here with my things packed in two hours. At twelve-thirty on the dot you must be ready, and waiting for me. Can you do that?

CATHERINE: I can do anything, my dearest!

MORRIS: Now! We must think carefully of how we shall word your letter.

CATHERINE: What letter?

MORRIS: The letter you leave for your father. Shall I write it for you? Shall I help you to write it?

CATHERINE: No.

MORRIS: You must be very clever in it. You must melt his heart. You must make him feel your love and affection!

CATHERINE: I am not going to write him.

MORRIS: Why, of course, we will write to him! We want him to forgive us!

CATHERINE (*backing away from him*): No, Morris, Please don't. He won't forgive us, ever. I know that now; I have good reason to.

MORRIS (*startled*): What reason?

CATHERINE (*hesitates a moment*): My father doesn't like me.

MORRIS: Why, what an unhappy thing to say! You must not think such things!

CATHERINE: It is true.

MORRIS: No, Catherine, your father is disappointed that his plans for you have not turned out as he wanted. He is perhaps hurt, and angry at us both. But that will pass.

CATHERINE: No, Morris, it won't pass.

MORRIS: My dear, if I am to be your husband you must begin to trust my judgement, to rely on me.

CATHERINE: Yes, Morris, I do.

MORRIS: That's right. How often do you think fathers have spoken angrily to the daughters they love, particularly when marriage is the question?

CATHERINE: He does not love me.

MORRIS: Of course he does! Indeed he must love you very much, or he would not be trying so hard to protect you. It is only your future happiness he is thinking of.

CATHERINE: No, Morris. In this one thing I know I am right. I couldn't say it unless I were sure. I understood it tonight for the first time in my life. You can tell when a person speaks to you as if —

MORRIS: As if what?

CATHERINE: As if they despised you!

MORRIS: *Despised!*

CATHERINE: Morris, we must be very happy ... and you must never despise me.

MORRIS: Oh, Catherine, of course not!

CATHERINE: We must never ask him for anything. Never expect anything from him. We must be very happy and rely on him for nothing!

MORRIS: No ... No ...

CATHERINE: I will try to be the best wife in the world.

MORRIS: I know you will. I know you will. (*He is restless.*) Was that a noise?

CATHERINE: Was it my aunt?

MORRIS: I think I'd better go.

CATHERINE: I will get ready immediately.

MORRIS: Yes, you had better.

CATHERINE: I'll try to be punctual, Morris. I know you like that.

MORRIS: Till twelve-thirty, then — (*He starts for the hall.*)

CATHERINE (*stopping him*): Morris, aren't you going to embrace me?

MORRIS (*smiles and takes her in his arms. They embrace warmly*): Oh, Catherine dear. He can't dislike you that much! He's bound to come round.

CATHERINE (*holding him at arm's length*): No, Morris, even if *he* would, *I* would not.

MORRIS: I see. (*He prepares to leave*): Until later, my dear.

He goes out quickly to the back of the house. CATHERINE *is in a state of exaltation. Her arms reach out to him after he has left, then she recovers herself. She goes to the mirror over the mantel and is pleased and even a little vain at what she sees. Then, remembering all she has to do, she picks up her skirts and runs upstairs as —*

THE CURTAIN FALLS

To indicate a passage of time

When the curtain rises, the room and house are dark, except for a flicker of light from the fireplace. A dark figure rustles down the stairs, carrying a candle. It is Catherine. She has a bonnet and travelling coat over her dress of the last scene. She puts down the little bag, next to the luggage in the hall, and then lights the candle which she has held in the other hand. Now she goes back to the stairs, and gets another small bag, which she places on her lap when she sits down. She puts the candle on the table next to her. She is hot with excitement and uses her handkerchief to wipe her forehead and neck. The sound of a carriage passing in the street is heard. CATHERINE *rushes to the window, opens it. The breeze blows the curtains into the room. She stands there. A church clock across the Square chimes the half-hour.*

MRS PENNIMAN, *in a dressing-gown and sleeping-cap, also holding a candle, comes down the stairs. When she sees Catherine in the chair she hurries into the room.*

MRS PENNIMAN: Catherine!

CATHERINE: Shh!

MRS PENNIMAN: What are you doing?

CATHERINE: Aunt Penniman, I would like it if you would please go back to bed.

MRS PENNIMAN: I want to know what you are doing!

CATHERINE: I am eloping with Morris.

MRS PENNIMAN: That's impossible! It's for tomorrow —

CATHERINE: Shhh! (*She stands up, gathers her bag in hand and runs back to the window.*)

MRS PENNIMAN: No, no, you have got everything wrong! You have misunderstood him. This is not right; he will be here tomorrow afternoon!

CATHERINE (*smiling at her*): No, Aunt, he will be here in the next fifty seconds. (*She laughs exultantly.*)

MRS PENNIMAN: Oh! Why didn't you tell me?

CATHERINE: He only slipped away an hour or so ago. I have had to re-pack all that Maria unpacked. It was hard work. (*She laughs again.*) But it was worth it!

MRS PENNIMAN (*excitedly*): Will you spend the night with him *unwed?*

CATHERINE: We will go to the Reverend Lispenard's directly. If he will marry us perhaps we may stay with him. If not, we will drive all night. I don't care!

MRS PENNIMAN: Oh, Catherine, how romantic, how wonderful for you! Morris is so daring . . .

CATHERINE: Shh! I think I heard a carriage — (*They listen for a moment.*) No . . .

MRS PENNIMAN: Catherine, wouldn't you like me to dress quickly and come with you.

CATHERINE: No, Aunt, there's no time. Morris will be here any instant.

MRS PENNIMAN: I think I should, Catherine. If you do have to drive all night, you must have a chaperone. Your father would be shocked —

CATHERINE (*she laughs*): It serves him right.

MRS PENNIMAN (*hardly believing her ears*): It serves who —?

CATHERINE: Father . . . he finds me so dull. It will surprise him to have such a dull girl disgrace his name.

MRS PENNIMAN (*comes closer*): Catherine, are you quite yourself?

CATHERINE: There it is —

They listen again for the sound of a carriage.

MRS PENNIMAN: No, it is a box blowing in the wind.

CATHERINE: To think I may never stand in this window again! That I may never see Washington Square on a windy April night!

MRS PENNIMAN: Why won't you?

CATHERINE (*surprised at the question*): Because I will never be in this house again.

MRS PENNIMAN: Nonsense!

CATHERINE (*gravely*): No, Aunt, it is not nonsense.

MRS PENNIMAN: You will be reconciled with Austin within the year. I guarantee it!

CATHERINE: You had better not do that. I will never see him again in my life.

MRS PENNIMAN: *What?*

CATHERINE (*crossing to the clock*): What is the time? Twenty-five to one?

MRS PENNIMAN: Catherine, come here! I want you to tell me what you mean.

CATHERINE (*simply*): I am leaving tonight instead of to-morrow, because it is one time less that I will ever have to lay eyes on him. Or he on me. We dislike each other too much, Aunt. It is bad for both of us, now.

MRS PENNIMAN (*gasps*): But, good God, child, you're dis-inheriting yourself!

CATHERINE (*serenely*): Yes . . . completely.

MRS PENNIMAN (*horrified*): Have you told Morris this?

CATHERINE: Of course. I told him everything.

MRS PENNIMAN: Oh, you didn't! You shouldn't!

CATHERINE: Why shouldn't I?

MRS PENNIMAN: Oh, Catherine, even if you felt as you did about your father, why did you tell Morris *now?*

CATHERINE: I had to tell him now. He is to be my husband!

MRS PENNIMAN: You should have waited. You should have waited until you were married!

CATHERINE: We will be married tonight.

MRS PENNIMAN: Did he . . . did he understand?

There is the sound of a carriage in the street.

CATHERINE: There he is! (*Feverishly she gathers up her two bags, shawl and gloves.*) Good-bye, Aunt! (*She runs to the hall.*)

MRS PENNIMAN (*excited*): Catherine —

CATHERINE: I will write to you.

She runs to her and gives her a small bag that CATHERINE

forgot. CATHERINE *laughs and goes out.* MRS PENNIMAN *goes to the window. The sound of the carriage increases as it nears the house. Then it recedes as the carriage continues on its way.* MRS PENNIMAN *turns away from the window. After a pause we hear the front door close, and then* CATHERINE *comes back into the parlour.*

CATHERINE: It went by — (*She sits down on the small settee. The tower clock chimes the three-quarter hour.* CATHERINE *listens to it.*) Aunt, why shouldn't I have told Morris?

MRS PENNIMAN: Oh, dear girl, why were you not a little more clever?

CATHERINE: Clever? About what?

MRS PENNIMAN: About your father's money – about Morris –? Oh, Catherine, if you have spoiled this opportunity . . .

CATHERINE: *Spoiled!* In one hour from now Morris and I will be married. (*Rises and goes to mantel.*)

MRS PENNIMAN: I hope so.

CATHERINE: *Hope!* (*With a nervous laugh she looks at the clock.*) He is only fifteen minutes late! You are ridiculous!

MRS PENNIMAN: No, I am not, Catherine. I know him so well . . .

CATHERINE (*outraged*): *You* know him! *I* love him!

MRS PENNIMAN: Morris would not want to be the cause of your losing your natural inheritance. He could not see you impoverished.

CATHERINE: Impoverished! We shan't be impoverished! I will have ten thousand dollars a year!

MRS PENNIMAN (*explaining uneasily*): For some people ten would be a great come-down. It would be like . . . like having none.

CATHERINE (*bewildered*): How could it be? It is a great deal of money!

MRS PENNIMAN: Not when one has expected thirty.

CATHERINE: Morris has expected nothing! (*Desperately trying to explain it.*) He loves me! He wants me for his wife!

MRS PENNIMAN: He would never allow a wife of his to live in an undignified manner.

CATHERINE (*rebelliously*): What is undignified about it? We have more than Marian and Arthur had.

MRS PENNIMAN: Yes, Catherine, but Marian was one of the most popular girls of her year . . . She was a beauty . . . She was a belle . . .

CATHERINE (*outraged*): You think what my father thinks! You think I am dull and ugly! Well, you are wrong! Morris loves me! (*As if quoting.*) I am everything he ever yearned for in a woman.

MRS PENNIMAN (*sympathetically*): Oh, Catherine . . .

CATHERINE: I am! I am! He has told me so! *He* thinks I am pretty! He wants me! He could not wait for tomorrow night! He said we must go tonight! . . . (*She remembers the truth with anguish.*) No – I said that, didn't I? I said we must go tonight — (*With sudden hope.*) But he agreed! He was willing! You can see that for yourself. He was very willing . . .

MRS PENNIMAN (*hopefully*): Perhaps he will come.

CATHERINE: *Perhaps?* Oh, my God! – Don't say that to me!

MRS PENNIMAN: What am I to say?

CATHERINE: I can't bear it! I cannot bear it another minute! He *must* come! He must take me away! He must love me!

MRS PENNIMAN (*she hurriedly closes the sliding doors*): Catherine, you must control yourself!

CATHERINE: No one can live without that! You can't bear it in the end. . . . Someone must love me, someone must tell me he wants me. I have never had anyone! (*She tears off her cloak.*)

MRS PENNIMAN: Catherine, dear, you are hysterical.

CATHERINE: Morris is the only one! I have never heard tenderness in anyone's voice but his!

MRS PENNIMAN: I don't think you should say that.

CATHERINE: Why not? Am I not supposed to know it? Am I too dull? That's what my father thinks. He thinks if you are stupid you don't feel! That is not true, Aunt. I am very stupid, but I have felt everything . . . I used to think my misfortune was that mother died; I don't think that any more. She was so clever, that if she had lived, she, too, could not have loved me! (*She puts her head down now and weeps.*)

MRS PENNIMAN: Catherine, you must take hold of yourself!

CATHERINE (*moaning*): No, Morris must take hold of me! Morris must love me — (*She weeps again.*) Morris must make up for all those who haven't.

MRS PENNIMAN: Catherine, dear, I have explained it to you. I have told you why he might not come.

CATHERINE: You have not told me how I shall go on living if he doesn't!

MRS PENNIMAN: You have your father and me, my dear.

CATHERINE: I have nothing! I have always had nothing! And if Morris has tricked me, then I know that no one has ever loved me in my life. And no one ever will! (*As she says this, the clock strikes one. She listens, and then she breaks down completely.*) Oh, my God! My God! (*She bends over, racked with pain.*)

MRS PENNIMAN (*softly*): Catherine . . .

CATHERINE: Leave me alone, Aunt. Please leave me alone . . .

MRS PENNIMAN (*trying to quiet her*): There will be other young men.

CATHERINE: They would only want what he wants. And I don't want them. I will love him all my life . . .

MRS PENNIMAN: You will not let yourself be consoled!

CATHERINE (*rocking dully*): No, not consoled — Loved, Aunt, but not consoled.

> *She falls over on the couch.* MRS PENNIMAN, *helpless, kneels on the floor beside her.*

CURTAIN

The same. A rainy morning three days later. As the curtain rises there is a knock on the front door, and a tinkle of the bell at the back of the house. The room is cold with the light of a grey morning.

MARIA *enters from the kitchen and goes to the front door.*

MARIA (*opening the door. We hear the voices. Off-stage*): Yes?

MAN'S VOICE (*off-stage*): Is Dr Sloper in, miss?

MARIA (*off-stage*): Yes.

MAN'S VOICE (*off-stage*): Will you ask him to come across the Square to Mrs de Rham's, miss?

MARIA (*off-stage*): Dr Sloper is ill. He isn't making any calls.

MAN'S VOICE (*off-stage*): She's been taken awful bad and we need the doctor right away.

MARIA (*off-stage*): I'm sorry, but Dr Sloper has been laid up for three days himself.

MAN'S VOICE (*off-stage*): What am I to do?

MARIA: Try Dr Isaacs in Great Jones Street.

MAN'S VOICE (*off-stage*): She wants Dr Sloper, miss.

MARIA: I'm very sorry. Good morning.

She closes the door, then stands hesitant at the foot of the stairs.

MRS PENNIMAN *enters from the kitchen.*

MRS PENNIMAN: Who was that, Maria?

MARIA: It was the de Rham's coachman, ma'am. Mrs de Rham is ill. They want Dr Sloper.

MRS PENNIMAN: Oh, the Doctor can't go out.

MARIA: I know, ma'am. I told them to get Dr Isaacs.

MRS PENNIMAN: That was quite right, Maria.

MARIA: Do you think I should tell the Doctor about Mrs de Rham? I don't like to disturb him.

MRS PENNIMAN: Oh, he's awake. (MARIA *starts upstairs.*) He's dressing. You have more influence with him than I. You might tell him that it is unwise to come downstairs.

MARIA: Yes, ma'am. (CATHERINE *comes down the stairs.*) Good morning, miss.

CATHERINE: Good morning, Maria.

MRS PENNIMAN: Good morning, Catherine.

CATHERINE: Good morning, Aunt.

She watches Mrs Penniman with the mail. MARIA *goes up the stairs.*

MRS PENNIMAN: No, there is nothing, Catherine. They are all for your father. (CATHERINE *goes to the window and stares out. Her* AUNT *regards her anxiously.*) Catherine, dear, won't you let me get you some breakfast? (CATHERINE *does not reply.*) I don't know how long you can go on in this way, Catherine, without food or sleep. I know you were awake most of the night.

CATHERINE: I'm sorry, Aunt, if I disturbed you.

MRS PENNIMAN: You didn't disturb me. I'm just afraid that you are going to be ill.

CATHERINE: Ill?

MRS PENNIMAN (*nervously*): Yes. And with your father ailing . . . He asked for you again this morning. I do wish you would go in to see him.

CATHERINE: I don't want to see him.

MRS PENNIMAN (*she watches as* CATHERINE *goes through the mail*): Catherine, dear, I told you they are all for your father.

CATHERINE: Yes, I know. (*She goes through them just the same.*) Aunt Penniman, supposing Morris were ill?

MRS PENNIMAN: Morris?

CATHERINE: Yes.

MRS PENNIMAN: Oh, Catherine . . .

CATHERINE: Suppose it were something quite sudden?

MRS PENNIMAN: I don't think —

CATHERINE: If he were ill, he couldn't write, could he?

MRS PENNIMAN: Wouldn't he have sent some word?

CATHERINE: He is alone; he has no one to send!

MRS PENNIMAN: He has his sister.

CATHERINE: But our plan was a great secret. He has not dared confide in her.

MRS PENNIMAN: Catherine, dear, there are many ways of sending you word.

CATHERINE (*with mounting conviction*): That is not true, Aunt. My father is ill and *he* could not send a message if *we* refused to take it.

MRS PENNIMAN: Why would his sister refuse him such a thing?

CATHERINE: Mrs Montgomery did not like me. Morris could well think that I have deserted *him*. That's it! There he lies alone and ill, and for three days I have done nothing.

MRS PENNIMAN (*helplessly*): I can't bear to see you torturing yourself.

    DR SLOPER *is heard coming down the stairs.* MARIA *is behind him, carrying his coat. He is fully dressed, but wears a quilted dressing-gown over his suit.*

MARIA: But, Doctor, I don't think you should be up at all.

DR SLOPER: Well, I do. Now stop fluttering about, Maria. I am perfectly well able to walk downstairs. (*He comes into the drawing-room and sees the two women.*) Good morning, Catherine. (*No reply.*) . . . Lavinia.

MRS PENNIMAN: Good morning, Austin.

CATHERINE: Good morning, Father.

DR SLOPER: I haven't seen much of you ladies the last few days . . . (*To Maria.*) Get my things, Maria. (*He takes off his dressing-gown.*)

MARIA: But Doctor, it's starting to rain again. And I'm sure Dr Isaacs will be there right away.

DR SLOPER: So shall I. Get my bag.

MARIA (*frustrated*): Oh, Doctor!

DR SLOPER: And in the top of that medical box in my

study you'll find a black instrument. Bring that with my bag.

MARIA: Yes, Doctor . . . (*She goes out.*)

MRS PENNIMAN: It's a raw morning, Austin. Better dress warmly. (*She pulls her shawl around her.* DR SLOPER *notices it.*)

DR SLOPER: Are you pleased with your shawl, Lavinia?

MRS PENNIMAN: Oh, very much, Austin! You couldn't have brought me a nicer present.

DR SLOPER: Catherine, did Aunt Elizabeth like her silver tray?

CATHERINE: I don't know.

DR SLOPER: But she knows we are back, doesn't she?

CATHERINE: I don't know.

DR SLOPER: You mean to say you didn't send her word?

CATHERINE: No.

DR SLOPER: But I was ill, Catherine! You might at least have done that! (CATHERINE *does not answer.* DR SLOPER *turns to Mrs Penniman.*) And you, Lavinia, were you too busy to let Elizabeth know we were home?

MRS PENNIMAN: Catherine wanted a few days to rest. (*An inspiration.*) To get over her seasickness.

DR SLOPER: Catherine was not seasick.

MRS PENNIMAN: Excuse me, Austin, I must go to market. (*She goes out.*)

DR SLOPER: Well, Catherine, I have not seen you for three days. You have obviously avoided me. I understand by that that your departure is imminent. It would be a convenience to me to know when I may expect an empty house. When you go, your aunt marches. Is it tomorrow?

CATHERINE: No.

DR SLOPER: Is it next week?

CATHERINE: No.

DR SLOPER: The week after?

CATHERINE: I don't know.

DR SLOPER: Has he asked you to keep your plans secret from me?

CATHERINE: No . . . Will you excuse me, Father? (*She makes an agonized attempt to get out of the room.*)

DR SLOPER: Come here a moment, Catherine. Here in the light. (CATHERINE *reluctantly does so.* DR SLOPER *looks at her closely.*) You are flushed. Have you a little fever?

CATHERINE: No.

DR SLOPER: Your eyes look sick. Have you been weeping? (*She does not answer.*) Oh, Catherine! (*Still no answer.*) . . . (*A pause.*) Have you . . . have you broken your engagement . . . ? (CATHERINE *bows her head.*) If you have, I must tell you, Catherine, that I admire you greatly for it. (*She does not answer.*) It was a most courageous thing to do. (*He takes her by the shoulders.*) I understand your feelings. I know the effort you must have made.

CATHERINE (*barely audible*): Do you, Father?

DR SLOPER: I see it is still painful for you to speak of it. I will not insist. In time, Catherine, the pain will pass, and you will see better how wise and how strong you have been.

MARIA *returns with bag and instruments.* DR SLOPER *takes them from Maria.*

CATHERINE (*almost blindly*): Excuse me, Father, I have some letters to write . . . (*She goes into the study.*)

DR SLOPER: Thank you, Maria.

MARIA (*puzzled, indicates the instrument as* DR SLOPER *stares after Catherine*): Is that a flute, Doctor?

DR SLOPER: It's a stethoscope. I got it in Paris. It's for listening to people's hearts . . . I wish I'd had one long ago. (*He tucks it under his arm. He goes to the hall.*) Maria, have something hot for me when I get back, will you?

MARIA: Yes, Doctor, but wouldn't you like me to come with you? I could carry the umbrella.

DR SLOPER: No. Stay here with Miss Catherine. Do what you can for her. I'm afraid she is deeply troubled.

MARIA: Yes, Doctor.

> DR SLOPER *goes to the front door.* MARIA *opens it for him. He goes out.* MARIA *closes the door and returns to the drawing-room, where she picks up Dr Sloper's dressing-gown.* CATHERINE *opens the door of the study.*

CATHERINE (*in the doorway*): Maria, will you do me a favour?

MARIA: Yes, miss.

CATHERINE: Has my father left?

MARIA: Yes, miss.

CATHERINE: I have a note here. It's for an address in the Second Avenue. It's very urgent. Would you take it for me?

MARIA: Yes, miss.

CATHERINE (*relieved*): I will add a line, Maria, while you get your bonnet.

MARIA: Very well, miss. (CATHERINE *goes back into the study, hastily closing the door.* MARIA *finishes tidying the room, then picks up the dressing-gown and prepares to take it to the back of the house. As she gets to the hall, the front doorbell rings.* MARIA *answers the door – off-stage.*) Good morning, Miss Marian.

MARIAN (*off-stage*): Good morning, Maria. Is it true that they are back?

MARIA (*off-stage*): Yes, ma'am, they got in Sunday night.

MARIAN (*entering*): So I heard, and I am so provoked about it! I did want to meet them. Someone should have told us!

MARIA: Well, ma'am, your uncle has not been well, and there was a great deal of unpacking to do. I'll tell Miss Catherine you are here. (*She knocks on study door.*) Miss Catherine, Mrs Townsend is here.

CATHERINE (*from study*): What?

MARIA: Townsend.

CATHERINE (*flinging door open*): Townsend! (*She enters. Stops short when she sees that it is not Morris.*)

MARIAN: Yes, I can't get used to being Mrs Townsend either!

(*Laughs and opens her arms to embrace Catherine.*) Welcome home, Cathie. How good it is to see you!

CATHERINE: Thank you, Marian. (*They embrace.*) Maria, will you be ready to take the note?

MARIA: Yes, miss, I'll just get my things. (*She goes out.*)

MARIAN: I should be angry with you, Cathie, but as long as you got home safely I will forgive you. Did you have a wonderful trip?

CATHERINE (*laughs*): Yes, it was wonderful.

MARIAN: And to think that Morris Townsend was here to greet you and *we* were not! I'll never get over it.

CATHERINE: Morris?

MARIAN: Yes.

CATHERINE: Have you seen him?

MARIAN: Yes, last evening. I was angry with him, too, for not telling us sooner, but he thought we knew.

CATHERINE: What did he say?

MARIAN: Not much of anything. He just came by to borrow the money for his passage. Arthur didn't want to give it to him. It's an expensive trip to New Orleans.

CATHERINE: New Orleans? When does he go?

MARIAN: He sailed last night at midnight.

CATHERINE: So he has gone?

MARIAN: Yes. From there he goes to California. He is convinced he will find gold in California.

CATHERINE (*with the first show of strength*): He will go to great lengths to find it.

MARIAN: I hope he does, for I want him to pay Arthur back. (*Shyly.*) It is costly, having a baby nowadays.

CATHERINE: A baby? Oh, Marian! how pleased you must be.

MARIAN: Oh, yes! I am! I am!

MARIA (*enters*): I am ready, Miss Catherine.

CATHERINE: Yes, Maria?

MARIA: For the errand I am to go on. You said it was urgent.

CATHERINE: Oh, that! It is no longer urgent, Maria.

MARIA: Then I'm not to go now, miss?

CATHERINE: No, Maria.

MARIA: Thank you, miss. (*Goes out.*)

MARIAN: Tell me about Paris. Where did you buy most of your things?

CATHERINE: At Madame Talman's.

MARIAN: Oh, how wonderful!

CATHERINE (*with deliberate irony*): She made me everything. Evening clothes, cloaks, and street dresses. And I bought a great deal of every kind of under-linen.

MARIAN (*excitedly*): It sounds wonderful! It's a trousseau for a princess!

> CATHERINE *quietly tears up the note she has held in her hand.*

CATHERINE: Yes, it is.

MARIAN: And it's so sensible. Any time you decide to marry, you will have everything you need.

CATHERINE: Yes, Marian. There is a shop in Paris where they make only baby things. I bought a great deal there, too.

MARIAN: Oh, how sweet of you!

CATHERINE: I bought things in different sizes and both pink and blue trimmings.

MARIAN: That was wonderfully thoughtful. Mother must have written you.

CATHERINE (*after a pause*): I want you to have everything.

MARIAN: Cathie, dear! Of course, there is nothing you could have brought me that I would appreciate more!

CATHERINE: Would you like to see the baby things? I have them unpacked . . . They are in my room.

MARIAN: Oh, I'd love to!

CATHERINE: If you'll come upstairs with me and I'll show them to you.

MARIAN: I will take very good care of everything. And some day I will give them all back to you.

CATHERINE *takes* MARIAN *by the hand and leads her into the hall.*

CATHERINE: No; I will never need them.

MARIAN: Why, of course you will!

DR SLOPER *enters from the front door.*

DR SLOPER: Marian.

MARIAN: Uncle Austin.

DR SLOPER: What a cheerful surprise!

MARIAN *goes to him and kisses him.*

MARIAN: Welcome home. How are you? (*She stands off and looks at him.*) Are you not well?

DR SLOPER: I'm fine, fine, But you . . . how are you?

MARIAN (*laughing a little shyly*): Well, I . . . I am blooming.

DR SLOPER: Oh, good! And when are you going to pay me a professional visit?

CATHERINE (*interrupting*). I'll be in my room, Marian (*She goes up the stairs.*)

MARIAN: Yes, Catherine. (*Turns back to Dr Sloper.*) When would you like me to?

DR SLOPER: Come see me day after tomorrow.

MARIAN: I will.

DR SLOPER: How is your mother?

MARIAN: She is very well, and she will be happy to know that you are home. (*Remembering the time.*) I must hurry back, Uncle Austin, but first I want to see Cathie's Paris finery.

DR SLOPER: By all means! And, Marian, come and see her as often as you can, will you?

MARIAN: Yes, of course I will. (*Goes up the stairs.*)

DR SLOPER *sits down wearily.* MARIA *enters and quietly takes his things from him. She puts his bag on the table. The stethoscope sticks out of it.*

MARIA: How was Mrs de Rham?

DR SLOPER: I don't know, Maria; I didn't get that far . . . I felt quite faint. I lurched against the railing. (*Puzzled.*) I had a little difficulty getting back up our steps.

MARIA (*scolding*): You should have stayed in bed, Doctor. You got up too soon!

DR SLOPER: Yes, that's probably it. (MARIA *picks up his bag and prepares to go into the study with it.*) Just a moment. (*He takes the stethoscope out of the bag.*) I want the . . . flute.

DR SLOPER, *left alone, proceeds to listen to his chest methodically and carefully just as if he were examining a new patient. While he is intent upon it,* MARIAN *and* CATHERINE *come from upstairs.*

MARIAN (*from the archway*): Uncle Austin, I'd love to spend a little time and talk to you, but I *must* hurry home. Arthur's mother is coming to lunch.

DR SLOPER: Yes, yes, I quite understand.

MARIAN (*kissing Catherine*): Cathie dear, I can never thank you enough for those lovely things.

DR SLOPER: Marian! Ask your mother to come by and see me, will you.

MARIA *re-enters from the study.*

MARIAN: Yes, Uncle Austin, I will. (MARIAN *goes to the front door, followed by* CATHERINE. *There are more good-byes at the door.* CATHERINE *starts back upstairs after Marian leaves.* DR SLOPER *stops her as she passes the archway.*)

DR SLOPER (*calling out*): Catherine, will you come here a moment, please? Maria, I think that you both should know this. I am ill. It's not just a simple congestion. There are already rales in the lungs. I shall need very good nursing. It will make no difference, for I shall never recover, but I wish everything to be done as if I should. I hate an ill-conducted sick-room, and you will be so good as to nurse me on the hypothesis that I shall get well.

MARIA (*with emotion*): Perhaps you will get well . . .

DR SLOPER: I am never wrong about these things. Now, in a few days, you will need a doctor for me; get Dr Isaacs. If the street noises make me restless, see that tanbark is put down. And, Catherine, I don't want your Aunt Lavinia in

my room at all. Unless I should go into a coma. (*To Maria.*)
As to food, don't overload me, Maria. Keep me on slops.
You know, beef broth and gruel.

MARIA: Yes, sir. (*Her head is bowed.*)

DR SLOPER: Also, hook a large towel around both knobs of
my door, so that it doesn't close noisily.

MARIA: Yes, sir.

DR SLOPER: Find a small lamp; put fresh wicks in it so that it
doesn't smell. I want that kept lighted at all times. It is most
annoying fumbling around in a dark sick-room.

MARIA: Yes, sir.

DR SLOPER: Now if you will open up the bed for me, I'll be
there in a moment.

MARIA (*on the verge of tears*): Yes, sir.

CATHERINE: I will help you, Maria.

DR SLOPER: Catherine, Catherine will you sit with me a
minute, please?

CATHERINE: If you wish it, Father.

DR SLOPER: You have great emotional discipline, Catherine.

CATHERINE: No, Father.

DR SLOPER: Oh, I admire it. Perhaps we are more alike than I
thought.

CATHERINE: Perhaps.

DR SLOPER: I told you how brave I thought you, my dear.
Today, for the first time, I see that you have sound judgement, and the courage to carry it through. Seeing that has
made my . . . my present difficulty less important. I cannot
begin to tell you how proud of you I am, my dear.

CATHERINE: Are you, Father?

DR SLOPER: Deeply, most deeply proud!

CATHERINE: He jilted me!

DR SLOPER: What . . .?

CATHERINE: Morris jilted me!

DR SLOPER: Oh, Catherine . . .

CATHERINE: *Now* do you admire me?

DR SLOPER (*with compassion*): My poor child . . . (*He reaches out to her.*)

CATHERINE: Don't be kind, Father! It doesn't become you. He only took *your* estimate of me. You should be elated!

DR SLOPER: Catherine, I am mortally ill . . . Don't withhold your natural affection.

CATHERINE: I have no affection for you, Father.

DR SLOPER (*shocked*): Because I tried to protect you from Morris Townsend?

CATHERINE: No, I see now why you did that.

DR SLOPER: Ah, then you admit that I was right?

CATHERINE: No. You thought any clever, handsome man would be as bored with me as you were. And would love as little as you did. It was not love that made you protect me. It was contempt. Am I to thank you for that?

DR SLOPER: Some day you will realize I did you a great service.

CATHERINE: I can tell you now what you have done: you have cheated me! If you could not love me, you should have let someone else try.

DR SLOPER: Morris Townsend did not love you, Catherine.

CATHERINE: I know that, now, thanks to you.

DR SLOPER: Better to know it now than twenty years hence.

CATHERINE: Why? I lived with *you* for twenty years before I found out that *you* didn't love me. I don't know that Morris would have cheated me or starved me for affection more than you did.

DR SLOPER: You have found a tongue at last, Catherine. Is it only to say such terrible things to me?

CATHERINE: Yes, Father, this is a field in which you will not compare me to my mother.

DR SLOPER: Catherine, Catherine! Should I have let him ruin your life? I think you are fortunate. You will meet some honest, decent man some day, and make him very happy. You have many fine qualities . . .

CATHERINE (*interrupting*): And I will have thirty thousand dollars a year.

DR SLOPER: Yes. That should make it possible for you to choose with discretion.

CATHERINE: If I am to *buy* a man – I would prefer to buy Morris!

DR SLOPER: Don't say such things!

CATHERINE: Why? Does it humiliate you?

DR SLOPER (*violently*): Catherine, promise me . . . promise me you have done with him!

CATHERINE: No.

DR SLOPER: Why not? You know him to be a scoundrel!

CATHERINE: I will not promise.

DR SLOPER (*angrily*): Then I must alter my will!

CATHERINE: You should. You should do it immediately.

DR SLOPER: I will do it when I choose!

CATHERINE: That is very wrong of you. You should do it now while you can. (*She rises and goes to the small desk.*)

DR SLOPER: I will attend to it tomorrow.

CATHERINE: You may not be well enough tomorrow.

DR SLOPER: I – I spoke hastily. I wish to consider more carefully.

CATHERINE (*coming back to him, she holds the pen and a tablet of paper out to him*): What is there to consider? Since I am unwilling to promise, I should not enjoy your fortune.

DR SLOPER (*desperately*): I don't want to disinherit my only child!

CATHERINE: You want your money used for purposes you approve, don't you? *I* certainly should! If you leave it to the Clinic it will do what you wish it to do. If you leave it to me, you know in whose pocket it may end — (*She almost smiles.*)

DR SLOPER: Catherine, I am ill!

CATHERINE (*sits down, prepares to write it herself*): You had better tell me how you wish it worded.

DR SLOPER: No!

CATHERINE (*writing and speaking the words*): I, Austin Sloper, Surgeon, of 16 Washington Square, do hereby make my last Will and . . .

DR SLOPER (*sweeping the paper off the table*): Catherine, this is an absurdity! You can't want me to do it; I don't want to do it!

CATHERINE (*rising*): I know you don't. You want to think of me sitting in dignity in this handsome house, rich, respected, and unloved for ever. That is what you think I deserve. But I may fool you, Father. I may take your money and chase after Morris, and squander it all on him! . . . Which do you think I will do?

DR SLOPER: I don't know.

CATHERINE: Then you must decide, and act accordingly.

DR SLOPER: I can't. I don't know!

CATHERINE: Perhaps you will in time.

DR SLOPER: No, I shan't, for I shall be dead.

CATHERINE (*her head rises proudly*): That's right, Father. You'll never know, will you?

THE CURTAIN FALLS

A summer evening almost two years later. The drawing-room is the same, except that two embroidery frames stand near the windows. The room is not swathed for summer, but the large fern in the fireplace, and the use of fans by the women, bespeak the time of year.

When the curtain rises, MRS PENNIMAN *sits at her embroidery frame, alternately placing her stitches and fanning herself. She is far more coquettishly dressed than she has been previously, although she is still in full mourning. But her lace cap, her necklace and bangles, make her a rather dressy figure.*

MARIA (*enters with a tray of cold lemonade*): Here we are, ma'am. I didn't sugar it. Miss Catherine likes to take her own sugar.

MRS PENNIMAN: Good. Put it there, Maria. Is our ice lasting pretty well?

MARIA: I have it wrapped in burlap, but I'm afraid it'll be gone by the morning. Even the cellar is hot tonight.

MRS PENNIMAN (*fanning herself*): Would you and Cook like to take a stroll in the Square? Miss Catherine and I will want nothing more.

MARIA: Maybe we will, ma'am. A night like this Miss Catherine should be at the seashore.

MRS PENNIMAN: For the last two years she has been saying she prefers the Square to a fashionable beach.

MARIA: She always used to go when Dr Sloper was alive.

CATHERINE *comes down the stairs. In her large, placid way she is growing into a dignified and almost attractive woman. She is dressed in a filmy, pale dress, a little fussy perhaps, but effective and handsome. She carries a work-bag of wools, needles, etc.*

CATHERINE: I have found a whole batch of colours that might do. I hope the moths haven't been at them —

MARIA (*looks at her, surprised*): Why, Miss Catherine, you have changed into one of your Paris gowns.

CATHERINE: Yes, Maria.

MARIA: It is very lovely, Miss. And very becoming to you. You look quite handsome —

CATHERINE (*coldly*): It is the *coolest* dress I could find.

MARIA: It's such a hot night, miss, I thought Cook and I might take a breath of air in the Square. Do you mind?

CATHERINE: No, of course not.

MARIA: Thank you, miss. (*About to leave.*)

CATHERINE: And, Maria – you are as free in this house as I. When you want a small favour, there is no need to blandish me with false compliments.

MARIA (*surprised*): Miss Catherine! I said what I meant! You *do* look handsome . . . Doesn't she, Mrs Penniman?

MRS PENNIMAN: Yes, Maria.

CATHERINE: We will not discuss it. I know how I look. (*She sits down at her embroidery frame.*)

MARIA (*looks helplessly at Mrs Penniman*): Thank you, miss. (*To Mrs Penniman.*) Good night, ma'am.

    CATHERINE *pulls her frame to the window indicated by the little grilled balcony outside the window, opposite Mrs Penniman, and settles for her embroidery.*

CATHERINE: I enjoy my sampler now. It has come on beautifully this summer.

MRS PENNIMAN: Would you not have liked to leave the city for a while, Catherine?

CATHERINE: No, Aunt.

MRS PENNIMAN: But you are young, my dear. Resorts were meant for girls like you. And with your enlarged income you could have taken a lovely house by the sea.

CATHERINE: I prefer it here.

MRS PENNIMAN: It worries me you see so few people.

CATHERINE: I see the people I like.

MRS PENNIMAN: But it is not right; I should *make* you do the things I know are good for you.

CATHERINE (*puts down her needle*): Are you discontented, Aunt?

MRS PENNIMAN: I am content for myself, Catherine, but then *I* am set in my ways. I am getting to be an old lady.

CATHERINE (*soothingly*): Let me give you some lemonade; it will cool you. (*Pours a little for herself.*)

MRS PENNIMAN (*looks out of the window*): There are so many young couples in the Square. I like to see them.

CATHERINE: If you would like to go for a stroll, Aunt, I will come with you.

MRS PENNIMAN (*positively*): Oh, no, I don't want to go out!

CATHERINE: Are you tired of your embroidery?

MRS PENNIMAN (*she looks at the clock on the mantel*): No ... er ... it hurts my eyes a little. (*Hesitates a moment, then sits down.*) Catherine, I am going to say something that will surprise you.

CATHERINE: Pray do. I like surprises. And it is so quiet here now.

MRS PENNIMAN (*watching her*): Well, then, I have seen Morris Townsend. (CATHERINE *puts down her needle and there is a dead silence.* MRS PENNIMAN *continues hurriedly.*) I met him by accident at Marian's. He has only been home a week. (*There is no sign from* CATHERINE.) He left there when I did, and we walked a little together. He is very handsome, but he looks older and he is not so animated as he used to be. There is a touch of sadness about him – I'm afraid he has not been very successful in California. (CATHERINE *is still silent.*) Catherine, dear, are you listening to me?

CATHERINE: Yes, Aunt.

MRS PENNIMAN (*gathering courage*): He asked ever so many questions about you, Catherine. He heard you hadn't married. He seemed very interested in that. He hasn't married, either.

CATHERINE: Please say no more.

MRS PENNIMAN: But I must, my dear! He sent you a message and I promised to deliver it. You must let me keep my promise.

CATHERINE (*with some anger*): I am not interested in your promises!

MRS PENNIMAN (*pleading*): Catherine, he wishes to see you! He believes that you never understood him – never judged him rightly, and the belief has weighed on him terribly!

CATHERINE: How can you bring me such a message? You stood in this room the night he deserted me!

MRS PENNIMAN: Catherine! Don't say that! He did not desert you! Oh, if you would hear him out – if you would try to understand his side of it. He meant it nobly, really he did!

CATHERINE: I can hear that you have been with him. He has beguiled you again, and you talk like a fool!

MRS PENNIMAN: I don't care what you think of me, Catherine, I am convinced that you will be happier after you have seen him.

CATHERINE: You can save your breath, Aunt Penniman. I will *not* see him!

The doorbell rings.

MRS PENNIMAN (*distraught*): Oh, dear!

CATHERINE: Who is that?

MRS PENNIMAN (*imploring*): Oh, Catherine —

CATHERINE (*in a stern voice*): Aunt Penniman, have you dared!

MRS PENNIMAN: Have I done wrong? . . . I couldn't help it . . . I want your happiness so! It must be right that you see him – you see no one, Catherine. Nor does he . . . I believe in love like that. If you are angry at me, don't be! I am not sensible, I know that, but I want to help . . .

CATHERINE: Aunt Penniman. Go to the door, and tell Mr Townsend I am not at home.

MRS PENNIMAN: Please —

CATHERINE (*firmly*): I am not at home.

MRS PENNIMAN *wilts and gives in. She goes to the hall.*

MRS PENNIMAN (*off-stage*): Good evening, Morris.

MORRIS (*off-stage*): Good evening, Mrs Penniman. (*At the sound of his voice,* CATHERINE *stiffens.*) It's a long time since I stood here.

MRS PENNIMAN (*off-stage*): Yes. I'm sorry, but Catherine is not at home.

MORRIS (*off-stage*): Oh . . .? Did you not give her my message?

MRS PENNIMAN (*off-stage*): Yes – but she is not at home.

MORRIS (*off-stage*): I see . . . (*A pause.*) I'm sorry.

CATHERINE (*calling out*): Come in, Morris.

MORRIS (*entering*): Good evening, Catherine.

CATHERINE: Good evening.

MORRIS: I have been sitting in the Square for the past half-hour watching your windows. I knew you were home. Do I offend you so by coming?

CATHERINE: You should not have come.

MORRIS: Didn't Mrs Penniman give you my message?

CATHERINE: I did not understand it.

MORRIS: It's easily understood, Catherine! I have never ceased to think of you.

CATHERINE: Morris, if you cannot be honest with me, we shall have nothing further to say to each other.

MORRIS: Very well, Catherine . . . I have ventured – I wanted so much to . . . May we not sit down?

CATHERINE: I think we had better not.

MORRIS: Can we not be friends again?

CATHERINE: We are not enemies.

MORRIS: Ah, I wonder if you know the happiness it gives me to hear you say that!

CATHERINE: Why have you come here to say such things?

MORRIS: Because since the night I went away it has been the

desire of my life that we should be reconciled. I could not break up your life with your father. I could not come between the two of you and rob you of your due.

CATHERINE: My father did not disinherit me, Morris! He threatened it, to test *you.*

MORRIS: But I could not be sure of that, the night I went away.

CATHERINE (*smiling*): No, you could not be sure.

MORRIS: And do you understand what my intention was . . .?

CATHERINE: I have had two years to think about it – and I understand it. So there is nothing further to discuss. I will bid you good night.

MORRIS (*shocked*): But I have come all the way from California to see you . . . to explain this to you!

CATHERINE: It is late for explanations.

MORRIS (*with growing desperation*): Oh, no, Catherine; I would have been back long since – but I have had to beg and borrow the passage-money! It has been a real struggle for me to get back here! Why, between New Orleans and Charleston I worked as a hand – a common seaman! Now that I am here you will give me the chance to vindicate myself . . . (CATHERINE *studies him.*) You must hear me out, Catherine! You must! (CATHERINE'S *expression does not change.*) Dismiss me later if you like, but hear me out now. For the sake of . . . for the sake of what we have been to each other, you must hear me out! Please!

CATHERINE: What is it you wish to explain?

MORRIS *breathes a sigh of relief.*

MORRIS: Many things, Catherine, many things – May we not sit down – now?

CATHERINE: Very well.

She goes to a chair. When she is seated, MORRIS *sits. There is a moment's silence as* MORRIS *appreciates his position.* CATHERINE'S *inquiring look forces him to speak.*

MORRIS: Sitting out there – (*indicating the window*) I knew just what I wanted to say . . . but seeing you, everything has gone out of my mind. You're changed, Catherine! You've grown into a handsome woman.

CATHERINE: Have I?

MORRIS: You are so serene.

CATHERINE: I live a quiet life. Perhaps that is why.

MORRIS: How blessed it must be to live like that, in this lovely house. I have been half across the world since I last sat here, and I tell you, Catherine, you are a lucky woman.

CATHERINE: Do you think so?

MORRIS: You have everything: security, position, wealth! No wonder you haven't married; you had nothing to gain by it.

CATHERINE: No, I had nothing to gain by it.

MORRIS: I have very little to offer you, Catherine, very little except my tenderest affection.

CATHERINE: Sometimes that is a great deal.

MORRIS: Catherine, it was *because* I loved you that I disappeared! I knew that if I returned that night, I might do you great harm.

CATHERINE: Is this what you have come back to tell me?

MORRIS: Oh, I know how it looked. It looked as if I behaved abominably, but that was not really the case. I had to be strong for both of us, and I refused to take advantage of your – feeling for me. You know, my dear, no man who really loves a woman could permit her to give up a great inheritance just for him. That is only in story books. (*Leaning towards her imploringly.*) Try to understand me, Catherine. Try not to think of what it looked like, but of what it really was. It was the expression of a husband's love, protecting a wife's future . . . Can you think of it that way?

CATHERINE: I will try.

MORRIS (*delighted*): You will! Ah, you're not implacable! Your aunt feared that you might be.

CATHERINE: My aunt does not know me very well.

MORRIS: Catherine, will you forgive me for the pain I caused you?

CATHERINE: I forgave you a long time ago.

MORRIS: Catherine, dear Catherine, we have only waited, and now we are free!

CATHERINE: How are we free?

MORRIS: Nothing stands between us.

CATHERINE: You mean you still love me?

MORRIS: I did not dare say it.

CATHERINE: Why not?

MORRIS: I wasn't sure you would believe me.

CATHERINE: I believed you once, didn't I?

MORRIS: It was true then, and it is true now, Catherine. I have never changed. And something tells me you have not, either.

CATHERINE: What tells you that?

MORRIS: Your expression – your forbearance with me. And the fact that I know you pretty well, and I know how deeply you feel.

CATHERINE: Do you, Morris?

MORRIS: Perhaps I sound fatuous, but I believe that your nature is such that you will always care for me a little.

CATHERINE: Yes, Morris, that is true.

MORRIS (*now ardent and hopeful*): Then let us waste no more time, my darling! Let us make the rest of life happy for each other!

CATHERINE: How?

MORRIS: How? Why, by picking up where we left off! By doing tomorrow or next week what we were going to do two years ago! By marrying, Catherine!

CATHERINE: Would you like that?

MORRIS: Like it! Catherine, you'd make me the proudest and happiest man in the world!

CATHERINE: And what would you make me?

MORRIS: I will try to be a good husband to you. I am older

and wiser now, and our marriage would mean a great deal more to me now.

CATHERINE: Why?

MORRIS: Because I know that you loved me and I have come to a place where I need that. I need it more than anything else.

CATHERINE *smooths the handkerchief on her lap, and folds it deliberately.*

CATHERINE: When would you like to marry me?

MORRIS (*rises and goes to her impulsively*): Oh, Catherine! Then you will!

CATHERINE: You are as persuasive as ever, Morris.

MORRIS: I mean to be! (*He turns her towards himself.*) Let us marry soon, very soon! After all, we have had our courtship.

CATHERINE: Yes, we have.

MORRIS: Next month?

CATHERINE: You are not as impetuous as you used to be.

MORRIS: Impetuous? Why, I would marry you tonight, if I could! (*There is a pause, and she looks at him.*) Would you, Catherine?

CATHERINE (*smiles*): Do you think the Reverend Lispenard is still waiting?

MORRIS (*laughing*): We could tell him we were detained ... Oh, Catherine, would you, really?

CATHERINE: I think I should like that.

MORRIS: Let us do it! Come with me now! We can find a carriage in the Square. Come as you are!

CATHERINE: You must give me time to pack.

MORRIS: Yes, of course.

CATHERINE: Where are your things?

MORRIS: At my sister's. We will pick them up on our way to Murray's Hill.

CATHERINE: Why don't you get them now, and then come back for me?

MORRIS: I will, my dear, I will run all the way to my sister's, and I will be back immediately.

CATHERINE: Do you remember the buttons I bought for you in Paris?

MORRIS: Oh, yes, the buttons.

CATHERINE: I have them still. Will you wear them tonight?

MORRIS: With great pride and love, my dear.

CATHERINE: I will get them. (*She starts to go out, at the door she calls.*) Aunt Penniman! Aunt Penniman! (*Turns back to the room and looks at the clock.*) We could be at Murray's Hill within the hour, could we not?

MORRIS (*looks at clock*): Yes, by ten. (CATHERINE *goes up the stairs.* MORRIS *watches her leave, then he turns back into the room and surveys his domain. He is drinking it in when* MRS PENNIMAN *enters.* MORRIS *turns, sees her, goes quickly to her and embraces her.*) I am home, really truly home!

MRS PENNIMAN (*anxiously*): What, Morris, what? . . .

MORRIS: She is magnificent . . .

MRS PENNIMAN *starts to smile.*

MRS PENNIMAN: Oh, I am so relieved!

MORRIS: She is superb. You have done a wonderful thing for me, Mrs Penniman.

MRS PENNIMAN: I've never stopped trying, Morris.

MORRIS: She has such dignity now.

MRS PENNIMAN: She is an admirable woman, really she is.

MORRIS: This time I am twice blessed. We are going to be married tonight.

MRS PENNIMAN: Then everything has come true! (*She starts to sniffle.*) Morris, you will be good to her, won't you?

MORRIS: I will cherish her the rest of my life.

MRS PENNIMAN: And I will see her in a happy home.

MORRIS: Yes. Yes . . .

MRS PENNIMAN: When is it to be?

MORRIS: We are leaving immediately.

CATHERINE *comes down the stairs.* MRS PENNIMAN *goes to her.*

MRS PENNIMAN: Catherine! Oh, my dear girl!

She tries to embrace her. CATHERINE, *kindly and smiling, keeps her away.*

CATHERINE: Thank you, Aunt. (*She hands the button box to* MORRIS.) Here they are, Morris. Your wedding present.

MORRIS (*taking it*): Thank you, my darling. (*He opens the box and looks in.*) Oh, Catherine, they are magnificent! They are rubies. Catherine, they are the most beautiful things I have ever had. Look, Mrs Penniman . . .

MRS PENNIMAN: Yes, I have seen them. They sparkle so! Oh, they suit you, Morris.

CATHERINE: Yes, they do.

MORRIS (*holds out his arms to her*): I shall cherish them all my life.

CATHERINE (*avoiding the embrace*): Not now, Morris. If we start kissing now we shall never get to the parsonage.

MRS PENNIMAN *laughs.*

MORRIS: No, no, I will hurry!

MRS PENNIMAN: How soon will you be back?

MORRIS: It will be a matter of minutes. Will you turn your head, Aunt Penniman? (*Smiling, she does so.* MORRIS *takes Catherine in his arms and kisses her.*) I will come as soon as I can, my dearest. We must not waste any more time — (*He picks up the box, and then, to dispel a last doubt.*) Catherine, you will have no regrets!

CATHERINE (*smiling*): No, Morris.

MORRIS: For a little while, then — (*He goes out quickly, taking his hat in the hall.*)

MRS PENNIMAN: Oh, Catherine, we have him back!

CATHERINE: Yes.

MRS PENNIMAN: I knew it would turn out this way. *You* were not so sure as I.

CATHERINE: No, Aunt. (*She goes towards the window.*)

MRS PENNIMAN: But I have faith in love like this. I hope I always stay romantic. And you know, Catherine, you are much more romantic than you think you are ... Morris sensed that —

CATHERINE: Yes, he did. (*She closes the window, and lowers the Venetian blind.*)

MRS PENNIMAN: Don't bother about that, dear, I will do it.

CATHERINE: There is no hurry, Aunt.

MRS PENNIMAN: He said he would be right back.

CATHERINE (*going towards the second window*): It will take him a little time. (*She closes this window and draws the curtains.*)

MRS PENNIMAN: I have so often read of things like this, and here it has come true in our own lives.

CATHERINE: Yes.

MRS PENNIMAN: That beautiful Paris lingerie ... how fortunate that you bought it. *I* am going to pack that for you. (*Archly.*) I will sprinkle it with fresh lavender. (*She makes a move to leave.*)

CATHERINE: Not yet, Aunt.

MRS PENNIMAN: But, dear, it's only a stone's throw to his sister's ... (CATHERINE, *finished with the window, goes to her embroidery frame and sits down at it. She picks up her needle.*) Oh, dear, you haven't time for *that*!

CATHERINE: I am just working on the 'Z'.

MRS PENNIMAN: Yes, I know, but don't do it *now!*

CATHERINE (*sewing*): I have only a few more stitches.

MRS PENNIMAN: You will finish it afterwards.

CATHERINE: No, Aunt, I must finish it now, for I shall never do another.

MRS PENNIMAN: That's right! You have better things to do.

CATHERINE: I have indeed! I can do anything now!

MRS PENNIMAN (*coaxing*): Come upstairs with me now, dear; you must look your prettiest.

CATHERINE: Sit down, Aunt.

MRS PENNIMAN: Oh, no —

CATHERINE: *Sit down!*

MRS PENNIMAN: But Catherine, Morris will be here . . .

CATHERINE: Morris will have to wait.

MRS PENNIMAN: What!

CATHERINE: He came back with the same lies, the same silly phrases . . . He thought I was so stupid that I would not detect his falseness. That proves that it is *he* who is stupid, and not *I!*

MRS PENNIMAN (*horrified*): No, no, Catherine! That is not true!

CATHERINE: He has grown greedier with the years. The first time he only wanted my money: now he wants my love, too. Well, he came to the wrong house, and he came twice. I shall see that he never comes a third time.

MRS PENNIMAN (*stricken*): Catherine, do you know what you're doing?

CATHERINE: Yes.

MRS PENNIMAN (*moaning*): Poor Morris . . .

CATHERINE: Aunt Penniman, if you ever mention his name again – if you so much as whisper it – I shall understand that you wish to live alone.

MRS PENNIMAN: Catherine!

CATHERINE: I shall take it as a sign that you are leaving Washington Square for ever.

MRS PENNIMAN (*frightened*): Catherine, can you be so cruel?

CATHERINE: Yes, Aunt, I can be very cruel. I have been taught by masters!

MRS PENNIMAN (*after a pause*): My dear, life can be very long for a woman alone – I am twice your age, and even I . . . even I . . .

CATHERINE: Good night, Aunt. (MRS PENNIMAN *goes out.* CATHERINE *sits at the frame and embroiders. We hear a carriage in the distance.* CATHERINE *listens to it. It grows louder and louder. In front of the house it stops. There is a pause and then the front doorbell rings.* CATHERINE *does not move. It rings again, and* MARIA *comes from the back of the house. As* MARIA *passes the drawing-room door,* CATHERINE *calls to her.*) I will attend to that, Maria. It's for me.

MARIA (*stops*): Yes, miss. (*The bell rings again.* CATHERINE *does not move.* MARIA, *puzzled, watches* CATHERINE *a moment.*) Miss Catherine . . .?

CATHERINE: Bolt it, Maria.

MARIA: Bolt it?

CATHERINE: Yes, Maria. (MARIA *goes to the door and slides the bolt. She waits a moment. A loud knock is heard.*) Good night, Maria.

MARIA: Good night, miss. (*She goes out.*)

CATHERINE *takes a final stitch, and then breaks off the wool thread. Now she rises and extinguishes the lamp that has lighted her sampler.* MORRIS *knocks again.* CATHERINE *goes into the hall and picks up the small lamp at the newel-post. There is another knock. As she starts up the stairs,* MORRIS *calls 'Catherine'. There are frantic knockings now, and under them we hear* MORRIS *again call: 'Catherine' –* CATHERINE *continues up the stairs, the light dims, and –*

CURTAIN